God's sovereignty and provide. the most important and foun.... .... of our faith. It is one that anchors us in times of trial. Jane Roach's study on Esther shows us God's providence in the life of an unlikely queen. This theologically rich study takes us through the pages of God's Word to see that all God's purposes come to pass
—**Christina Fox**, Author, *A Heart Set Free*

God's Mysterious Ways offers women a thought-provoking, heart-igniting exploration of God's quiet but invincible providence displayed in the life of Esther. Jane Roach's insightful study-and-discussion questions and clear exposition blend serious engagement with the scriptural text with a focus on Christ, our true Rescuer. Contemporary testimonies show what it looks like to live in the confidence that God works all things—both pleasant and painful—together for good to those whom he has called by grace in the gospel. Gather some sisters and work together through this study of Esther. It will move you to worship the Lord in awe at all times, and to rest in his sovereign wisdom and love in times of trial.
—**Dennis E. Johnson**, Author, *Walking with Jesus through His Word*

Jane Roach's Bible study on Esther is doctrinally rich and spiritually uplifting. This resource will be a tremendous aid to personal worship and devotional study, as well as for small group discussions. Discover God's providence in Esther and you will learn to see God's presence in your own life.
—**Richard D. Phillips**, Senior Minister, Second Presbyterian Church, Greenville

To have a robust and "no-risk" view of providence is essential for spiritual sanity, strength and stamina. Few books of the Bible teach rovidence with greater candor than Esther, and Jane Roach's no-nonsense approach, in ten accessible, practical chapters, provides an ideal manner of studying both the book of Esther and its central theme of providence. I foresee personal and group bible studies making this book their choice in the near future, and returning to it again and again. A marvelous aid that will do a great number of people much good.

    —**Derek W. H. Thomas**, Senior Minister, First Presbyterian Church, Columbia

God's Mysterious Ways

EMBRACING GOD'S PROVIDENCE IN ESTHER

Jane Roach

P&R PUBLISHING
P.O. BOX 817 • PHILLIPSBURG • NEW JERSEY 08865-0817

© 2016 by Jane Roach

All rights reserved. No part of this book may be reproduced, stored in a retrieval system, or transmitted in any form or by any means—electronic, mechanical, photocopy, recording, or otherwise—except for brief quotations for the purpose of review or comment, without the prior permission of the publisher, P&R Publishing Company, P.O. Box 817, Phillipsburg, New Jersey 08865-0817.

Unless otherwise indicated, Scripture quotations are from the ESV® Bible (The Holy Bible, English Standard Version®), copyright © 2001 by Crossway, a publishing ministry of Good News Publishers. Used by permission. All rights reserved.

Scripture quotations marked (NIV) are from the HOLY BIBLE, NEW INTERNATIONAL VERSION®. NIV®. Copyright © 1973, 1978, 1984 by International Bible Society. Used by permission of Zondervan Publishing House. All rights reserved.

Italics within Scripture quotations indicate emphasis added.

Quotations from The Expositor's Bible Commentary, Vol. 4 © 1988 by The Zondervan Corporation, *The Matthew Henry Commentary* © 2010 by Zondervan, *NIV Archeological Study Bible* © 2005 by The Zondervan Corporation, and *The Zondervan Pictorial Encyclopedia of the Bible* © 1975, 1976 by Zondervan Publishing House are used by permission of Zondervan. www.zondervan.com

ISBN: 978-1-62995-224-6 (pbk)
ISBN: 978-1-62995-225-3 (ePub)
ISBN: 978-1-62995-226-0 (Mobi)

Printed in the United States of America

To my heavenly Father,
who has opened my eyes to see his providence
and my heart to embrace it

Contents

Foreword

FOR THE SEARCHER, the seeker, there is a treasure to be found! It is as a diamond whose many facets combine with exquisite sparkling beauty and simplicity. Jesus spoke of it as a "treasure hidden in a field" (Matt. 13:44) and a "pearl of great value" (Matt. 13: 46).

What is this treasure of unspeakable radiance? It is the kingdom of God; it is the divine disclosure that God in Jesus Christ has leaped from the realms of glory and magnificence into our world of twistedness and blight. It is an altogether breathtaking reality that causes all others to pale in comparison. It is such that the grandeur of the great Grand Canyon—with ever-changing hues and designs endlessly repainted by the clouds across its undulating landscape—loses its shocking magnificence in comparison. What is initially spellbinding becomes a mere picture of the beauty and glory that alone belongs to God. What is this valuable treasure, this "pearl of great value"? It is the revelation to us that Jesus came into our world to change it forever; the evidence is enshrined, preserved, and protected for us in the Bible.

To have this great book is indeed a treasure, but it must be opened for us to experience its delights. This unique of all communications explains how God willed to redeem out of human lostness and tragedy a people for his own delight and possession.

As marvelous as that is, there is more. This great book tells us how to find comfort, instruction, and insight into how we are to live for him as we await the day when we shall see the one who loves us so profoundly. It tells us that the saving God is also one who preserves and protects his children, blood-purchased by his own dear Son; he is concerned not only that we come to him but also that we find our refuge in him, preserving us by his providential care so that "not a hair can fall from my head without the will of my Father in heaven" (The Heidelberg Catechism, Q.#1).

Among the many places in the Bible where this truth is illumined, perhaps there is none as gripping and vivid in story form as that in the book of Esther. What comfort to see and know that God cares for us, working all things according to his good pleasure.

I heartily commend this study guide, which comes from the hand and heart of a seasoned, godly exemplar of the truth.

John D. Hannah
Distinguished Professor of Historical Theology
Research Professor of Theological Studies
Dallas Theological Seminary
Dallas, Texas

Preface

WHO IS IN CHARGE? This is the fundamental question that the serpent posed to Eve and to every person since Eden. This question is in the forefront of our minds even when we are young. When one of my grandsons was three years old, his mother left him in my care at my home. As she was driving away, he put his hands on his hips, pulled back his shoulders, looked at me, and asked with an authoritative tone, "Well, who's in charge here?"

After I got over the shock, I got down to his level and looked him in the eye, replying, "You are not." He literally shook with surprise. We had a lovely conversation with him sitting on my lap as I explained that he was our guest and we were responsible for his care when he was with us. He was satisfied and we had a wonderful time together.

People still ask this same question in many different ways. Is there a God? If so, what is he like? Is God a person or a force? How does he relate to the world and people today? Is there objective truth? Are there objective standards? Does God have a Son? How many ways are there to salvation? What part does God play in evil? Who are the Jews and why is their history filled with efforts to eliminate them? Where is our world headed? What can we do to change the direction? Who decides the answers to these questions?

I have encountered people who answer these questions without a frame of reference outside of themselves. They sincerely believe mutually exclusive statements at the same time and see no contradiction. The need to know God as he has revealed himself in the Bible prompted me to teach a women's Bible study on the book of Esther, emphasizing the providence of God. It was delightful to encounter the class members in the community and hear them talking about God's providence, a topic previously not part of their conversations.

God is not mentioned in the book of Esther, yet it has many hints of his presence. The compelling narrative presents God as the all-powerful one who sovereignly directs history according to his predetermined plan. It has a message of hope for God's people in every age and culture.

While the world attempts to change the decrees of God the Creator, they will not succeed. God, not political leaders, will have the final say in what is right and wrong. God providentially watches over his people, and nothing and no one will ultimately prevail against them. In fact, those who attempt to destroy God's people find themselves fighting against God.

We might wonder where God is today. The spectacular gets our attention rather than the ordinary providence of God at work in our lives. Pop culture and the news celebrate those who assert their independence from God rather than the faithful who trust God day after day, in success and failure, sickness and health, joy and sorrow. Even in the professing church, people are often more concerned with what they have or do or appear to be than with who they are in Christ. When it seems God is nowhere to be seen, Esther provides a snapshot of our infinite God at work behind the scenes. God is already where we will be tomorrow. He is working out his divine plan for his glory and our eternal good. We need no "plan B"; God's perfect plan is being accomplished. This book invites you to take God at his Word in the mysterious fulfillment of all his promises. Its message is needed in the world today.

Esther is a book named after a woman, but it is part of God's revelation for all—men, women, and children. God reveals his providence that we may understand it and embrace it for our lives. To embrace means to cherish and hold dear. May you see and embrace God's providence in your personal life, your family, your church, your nation, and the world through taking a step back in time into the historical narrative of Esther.

Acknowledgments

GOD PROVIDENTIALLY brought people to teach me about him and his providence. My parents, other family members, Sunday school teachers, and a dear lady from my childhood church, Anna Mae Arnholt, were instrumental in my knowledge of God. As an adult, I was greatly influenced by A. Wetherell Johnson, Rosemary Jensen, James Montgomery Boice, John Hannah, and the writings of Elisabeth Elliot.

My husband, Jim, has often been a sounding board for me as I wrestled with ideas in this book and has prayed faithfully for me. My pastor, Dr. Allen Taha, has supported and encouraged me wholeheartedly throughout the process of writing this book. I am grateful for the people who have endorsed this book and encouraged me to write it. Thanks to Karen Smith and Linda Cress, who have read this manuscript, offering valuable ideas and corrections. Thanks to Debra Butts, who has read and reread and reread this manuscript, offering practical edits. God has providentially brought them into my life for such a time as this.

My longtime friend Carla Northington has graciously allowed me to teach the Bible study she has hosted for more than fifteen years. The women in this class have embraced the format of the study and, more importantly, the providence of God. The women of my church, Trinity Presbyterian in Boerne, Texas, diligently studied and openly shared their discoveries. Both groups of women have willingly shared their lives with me through our study of Esther, the fruit of which is this book. Their honest remarks have enriched my own understanding of God's providence. My friends and some of these class members have graciously agreed to tell their stories of God's providence in their daily lives, catastrophes, emergencies, joys, and sorrows. I am richer for knowing them during these times and for thinking through God's providential ordering of my own life. God works in mysterious ways as he makes himself known to his people.

Chad Swanson and Pat Macfarlane kindly helped with author videos and photographs. I am grateful to Amanda Martin, Julia Craig, and the entire P&R Publishing staff for their help and encouragement as well. To God be the glory for ordering my steps and opening doors for me. Great things he has done!

Introduction: Planning Ahead

ONE OF MY HOBBIES is counted cross-stitching. As I begin a piece, I look at the pattern, take inventory of the thread, and gather the necessary materials: light, frame, scissors, and other essentials for the project. I determine when I will stitch and when I will put it aside until the next opportunity. Too much at one time is not as profitable as smaller amounts at a measured pace. Allowing time to complete a gift before it needs to be wrapped and presented provides joy; rushing through to meet an imminent deadline guarantees mistakes that require pulling out threads and retracing steps. The project changes from pleasure to labor.

The same idea is helpful for other projects, including Bible study. I have found it helpful to study the Bible with some plan in mind. The plan is not law and should not degenerate into a checklist. It may vary some from day to day. However, a small daily taste with time to ingest and digest what I have read is better than a fire-hydrant gulp only once a week. I prefer to study in the morning, my best time of day. This morning routine gives me food for thought throughout the day. I prepare by having ready my Bible, paper, and pen to ask and answer questions about the text and by finding a place of solitude to read and pray as I study. I add to my study notes ideas I want to remember, other questions I want answered, and possible applications of the passage to my life. Allowing the text to ask questions of me further cements the truth of the passage in my mind and allows it to move into my heart and through my body—eyes, ears, mouth, hands, and feet.

The questions in this book are designed to provide a plan of study as well as the end result of knowledge about God that leads to embracing what he has revealed about himself. As you begin the study of Esther, let me encourage you to begin and end with God. A simple plan may help you get started. Read the pages of the lesson in the order they are presented in the text:

- Worship: Scripture text, truth, and hymn
  Use the text and hymn as the basis for worshipping God. Recount to him words of adoration related to what is revealed about him in the brief passage and hymn text. Sometimes, I read the hymn text without the music. Other times I sing the hymn text. Sometimes I do both.
- Word: Bible text and truth
  The Bible is God's word to you. Reading and pondering it is the most important part of each lesson.
- Wisdom: Opening prayer, questions, and commentary
  The opening prayer is an example of a simple prayer for God to direct your study and give you wisdom to understand and believe what you read.

  Answer the questions from the Bible before reading a commentary. The spaces allotted in the book are designed to help you. Some questions ask you to give the facts stated in a given passage. Others require you to draw conclusions about the truth that flows from those facts. Still others go another step to apply the truth to your life. Allow God to speak to you without the distraction of another's words. If you seem unable to answer a question, come back to it later. You may be surprised that you have been pondering it when you were not consciously thinking about it, and now you have an answer.

Read the commentary, including all the Scripture references. Remember, God's Word is most important. Highlight or underline helpful statements.

• Worship: Closing prayer

The closing prayer includes adoration of God as well as petitions for God's direction as you seek to implement the truth you have learned in your life. Write your own prayer that reflects what you have learned in the lesson.

The format of each chapter is also designed to be an aid to Bible teachers or leaders of groups. Perhaps you are saying, "Oh, I could never teach." God usually asks me to do something before I think I can, so that I depend on him. Esther's answer might work for you: "If I perish, I perish" (Esther 4:16). Living by faith is being on the cutting edge, and it is exciting!

Throughout the study, we will consider words of different hymn writers and also refer back to the hymn, "God Moves in a Mysterious Way." May you exult in the ways you see him moving in your life and respond with trust in him as your sovereign, powerful, providential, and personal God.

Embracing God's Providence

For from him [God] and through him and to him are all things. To him be glory forever. Amen. (Romans 11:36)

Texts

Genesis 1:1; Psalms 104:24–30; 139:16; Proverbs 21:1; and others related to God's providence.

Truth

God infallibly and sovereignly works to accomplish his plan.

Hymn: "Immortal, Invisible, God Only Wise"

Immortal, invisible, God only wise,
In light inaccessible hid from our eyes,
Most blessed, most glorious, the Ancient of Days,
Almighty, victorious, thy great name we praise.

Unresting, unhasting and silent as light,
Nor wanting, nor wasting, thou rulest in might;
Thy justice like mountains high soaring above
Thy clouds which are fountains of goodness and love.

To all, life thou givest, to both great and small,
In all life thou livest, the true life of all;
We blossom and flourish as leaves on the tree,
And wither and perish, but naught changeth thee.

Great Father of glory, pure Father of light,
Thine angels adore thee, all veiling their sight;
All praise we would render; O help us to see
'Tis only the splendor of light hideth thee!

—WALTER CHALMERS SMITH, 1867

Opening Prayer

O God, the immortal, invisible, and only wise God. You are hidden from my eyes and yet you have opened them to see your hand in providing for my practical needs, my longing for meaning, and my hope for the future, both temporal and eternal. You turn darkness into light and make rough places smooth. Please open my eyes to see your providence in my life. Teach me what your providence is, and enable me to embrace it in my life, my family and friends, my church, my nation, and the world. Great Father of glory, pure Father of light, help me see that only the splendor of light hides you from me. For your glory. Amen.

Questions for Study and Discussion

Question 11 of the *The Westminster Shorter Catechism* asks, "What are God's works of providence?" The answer states, "God's works of providence are, his most holy, wise, and powerful preserving and governing all his creatures, and all their actions."

God's Providence in Creation

▶ READ GENESIS 1:1

1. Describe God's relation to creation.

   He created the world to show His glory.

2. How would you explain God's purposes in creating the heavens and earth?

   God is glorified and beholds himself in his creation.

3. What is the definition of "providence"?

God providing protective or spiritual care.

Timely preparation for future eventualities.

Divine guidance or care.

God's Providential Care of His Creation

▶ READ PSALM 104:24–30

4. How are creation and providence related?

God created all things and He takes care of and provides for all things and creatures.

God's Providence over All of Life

▶ READ PSALM 139:16 AND PROVERBS 21:1

5. What do these verses reveal about God's providence in life and death?

He knew us before we were formed. The days of my life were prepared before I lived one day.

6. What part does faith play in embracing God's providence?

Faith replaces fear

7. How does God's providence show his personal care for his people? Give an example from your own life, if possible.

8. Does God providentially ordain evil? Explain your answer using any portion of Scripture.

9. What are some practical implications of believing in God's providence?

10. How does God's providence show you how to respond when things go poorly?

Commentary

I love it when my grandchildren come running and cling to me. That is what "embrace" means, is it not? You cling to what you know and love. Our opening prayer began, "O God." He is the reason we study the Bible. We study that we may know him as he has revealed himself in his Word. Because we will never know him fully, for he is infinite, we have a lifelong purpose—to strive to learn all we can about God. As we begin this study, we will seek to understand God's providence that we may then be able to recognize and embrace it both in the book of Esther and our own lives. We begin with God himself, the only true God.

Who God Is

He Created the World to Reveal His Glory

God alone is uncreated; he existed before matter, time, and space. God made the world by his powerful word (Psalm 33:6). All that he made exists by him, through him, and for him (Romans 11:36). We understand that our galaxy is but one of many; only God knows how many. What wisdom, what power our Creator has! All that God created is his and subject to him, the only self-existent being (Job 38:1–42:6). He is sovereign, highest in rank and authority. That is what it means to be God.

Why did he create the physical realm? The main reason is that God delights in revealing his perfect nature. Both angelic and human beings observe aspects of his character, such as his wisdom, eternal power, and divine nature in his creation (Romans 1:20). As they respond with reverence and awe, believing there is a Creator who fashioned the world out of nothing, God is glorified. God also beholds himself in his creation and is glorified.

The Creator Is Also the Sustainer of All

God did not create and then leave the world to its own ways. God designed each and every part of it—from the splendid galaxies to the minute nanoplankton—to fit perfectly into his creation, and he sustains them by his knowledge and power.

From spring until early summer, newborn fawns are dropped in our yard, where we enjoy watching them. By God's design, they have no scent until they are able to run fast enough to escape predators. If the doe stays with the fawn, her scent will attract the predators, so she leaves it alone. She returns periodically to nurse and clean it after scouting the area for danger. The fawn does not move until she signals it is safe. How she signals is not clear to me, but it seems to be a flick of her tail or a special sound. This is just one animal perfectly designed for its part in God's earth. Jesus said, "Look at the birds of the air: they neither sow nor reap nor gather into barns, and yet your heavenly Father feeds them. . . . Consider the lilies of the field, how they grow: they neither toil nor spin, yet I tell you, even Solomon in all his glory was not arrayed like one of these" (Matthew 6:26, 28–29). God receives glory as he sustains what he created.

The Apex of God's Creation Is Humanity

God created man and woman in his image so they could reflect his glory back to him. He sovereignly sets his affection on people according to his purposes and will. He guarantees that his purposes for each person and for all people will come to pass. Derek Thomas says, "Providence suggests God's care of the world, both his supervision of all events and circumstances *and* his provision for all of our needs. It is more than God's ability to 'see' into the future; it is his *active* and *determined* care to ensure that what he has promised for us actually does come to pass."[1]

God Has an Eternal Plan and Purpose for His Creation

God Has Purpose in What He Made, How He Made It, and Why He Made It

God has purpose in how he created each part of what he made. Above all, God's creation is to bring glory and pleasure to him. John Hannah credits Jonathan Edwards with the thought that God delights not in seeing his creation in itself but rather seeing himself in his creation.[2] His creation is to reveal his glory (the outshining of his perfect character), to display his eternal power and divine nature. His power is eternal because it acted before he created time. His creation reveals his divine wisdom, compassion, sovereignty, omnipresence, omniscience, holiness, justice, and providence.

God also created the earth to provide for the needs of his creatures: an inhabitable environment with temperate climates, food and water, breathable air for our lungs, beautiful sunrises, thunder and lightning, rain, trees and plants, and animals.

God created people to relate to him with truth, intimacy, joy, and love—to walk with him, talk with him, know him, enjoy him, praise him, thank him, worship him, and glorify him. To

1. Derek W. H. Thomas, *What Is Providence?*, Basics of the Faith (Phillipsburg, NJ: P&R Publishing, 2008), 6.
2. John D. Hannah, *To God Be the Glory*, Today's Issues (Wheaton, IL: Crossway, 2000), 19.

glorify means to call attention to his greatness, to point the spotlight on him by our testimony and by reflecting his character. Why do we not do that? God did not make robots. He gave the first human pair, Adam and Eve, responsibility to obey him out of love for him. He gave them everything they needed for life. He also gave them one prohibition—not to eat of a certain tree, lest they die. What did they do with this responsibility? They doubted his word and disobeyed him, wanting to be like him, deciding what was right and wrong for themselves. They usurped his authority over them as their Creator. They wanted to be "in control" of their lives.

Adam and Eve lost their freedom to serve God from a pure heart. They exchanged the inferior substitute of asserting their will for the infinite value and beauty of glorifying God. The beautiful, perfect relationship was over. They hid from him because they knew they had done wrong. They were alienated from him. All of their descendants, including us, fell with them. Adam and Eve's disobedience was no surprise to God. His plan to glorify himself and have a people specially related to him would not be thwarted by their disobedience.

Before God created the world, he had determined his plan of redemption. He predetermined how it would be played out for individuals, nations, and his specially chosen people. This is not plan B. God has always had only one plan. God immediately promised he would send a Redeemer descended from the woman (Genesis 3:15). He would remove his people's alienation from God and restore harmony with him. God designed his creation to glorify his eternal Son as the promised Redeemer who would redeem a people set apart for himself and set apart from sin. He is the main character of the entire Bible. He is both the eternal Son of God (God the Son) and the true man, Jesus of Nazareth.

History is his story. Through him, God displays his grace, mercy, and sovereignty toward undeserving people without sacrificing his holiness, justice, and righteousness.

The Bible Is the Record of God's Outworking of His Plan

The Bible tells us that God foreknew those who would be part of the people specially related to him. "Foreknew" in this sense does not mean knowledge of something before it happens; it does not mean that God looks forward and sees who will love him and thus he chooses them. "Foreknew" means that God set his affection on certain individuals before the creation of the world, before they even existed, much less did anything to merit his love. These individuals he "foreknew" in the special relationship with him for which they were designed but missed through sin, and he purposed and orchestrated his plan toward them. He gave these chosen ones to the Redeemer, his unique Son, as a special love gift (John 17). The purpose of his affection was to reconcile them to him in this life and to prepare them for the new heavens and earth that he would create in the future. In this new creation, there will be no evil and no temptation to sin because it will be a "sin-free" environment inhabited by "free-from-sin" people.

What God's Providence Is

God's Providence Is His Infallible Accomplishment of His Predetermined Plan

Infallible means perfectly in accord with his purpose and will. There is no room for error of any kind. God has knowledge in accord with his purposes for animate and inanimate things, individuals and nations, hours and ages, birth and death, catastrophes and calm, sun and rain, famine and feast, heaven and earth—whew! Nothing surprises God or escapes his notice. He is not restricted by our choices or actions, as though he needs to wait for us to make a move before he knows what to do in response to accomplish his plan. Some say that God is omniscient over all (knows everything) that has already happened, but he does not know everything in the future until he sees the choices of people. Then he responds to their choices or the consequences of those choices. (This puts people or "fate" in control of God rather than God in control of people and all things. Nothing could be further from the biblical teaching of God's omniscience, sovereignty, and providence.

God Knows What Needs to Happen and When for His Predetermined Purposes

Derek Thomas presents three views of God's providence.[3] The classical view is that God foreknows because he foreordains. This is the view on which this study is based. His will determines the future before any person ever acts (Ephesians 1:3–10). God is neither late nor early. He is always on time. He has "previously" been where we are today, preparing exactly what we need according to his predetermined purposes for us. It is not fate or fortune that determines what occurs in our lives. Neither is it solely our choices. Do not worry about tomorrow; God is already there.

When I was a teenager, I helped my father proofread work that he had typeset during the day. Thirty-five years later, when I started work at Bible Study Fellowship (BSF) headquarters,

---

3. Thomas, *What Is Providence?*, 17.

I was asked, "Do you proofread?" It was one of the "extras" I did there. God providentially prepared me in advance to be able to meet that need.

God Sustains and Governs in Accord with His Perfect Character and Will

God is love. He is all-wise and all-knowing, holy and perfect, merciful and just. He is good, righteous, infinite, immutable, incomprehensible, unsearchable, and omnipresent. He is not random, arbitrary, or chaotic. He is purposefully working toward his predetermined purpose and end for every part of his creation. We are not victims of chance or luck. The prophet Isaiah writes,

> Remember this and stand firm
> . . . .
> I am God, and there is no other;
>   I am God, and there is none like me,
> declaring the end from the beginning
>   and from ancient times things not yet done,
> saying, "My counsel shall stand,
>   and I will accomplish all my purpose,"
> calling a bird of prey from the east,
>   the man of my counsel from a far country.
> I have spoken, and I will bring it to pass;
>   I have purposed, and I will do it. (Isaiah 46:8–11)

God's Providence Is Both Gracious and Mysterious

We sometimes think we are free to do whatever we choose. But real freedom is having the will and power to do what God wills for us. Our plans mean nothing unless they align with God's plans. God graciously and mysteriously works his will in and through our choices. "For it is God who works in you, both to will and to work for his good pleasure" (Philippians 2:13). Even when our choices contradict his will and purposes, he is able to cause them to work toward his predetermined end (Romans 8:28–29).

If we are broken and not living as he purposed, is there a way to be restored to him? Yes, broken and lost people can be restored to God through faith in his Son, Jesus Christ, the Redeemer God provided. People already redeemed need renewed faith, strength, and power to live for his glory in an imperfect world that opposes him and tries to get rid of him. God works all things toward his end of making us like his Son so that we may have an intimate relationship with him through Jesus Christ.

Faith in God's Providence Has Practical Implications

Belief in God's providence has had some very practical implications for my life. I have included a few of my experiences to help you consider God's providence in your life.

Faith in God's Providence Replaces Fear with Confident Trust

I boarded an airplane ten days after September 11, 2001, to travel to Australasia to do God's work planned three years before the terrorist attack. Was God surprised by the attack? No! Was he directing my steps in accordance with his plan? Yes! What if I died? "For to me to live is Christ, and to die is gain" (Philippians 1:21). I boarded the plane, trusting God's providence. What causes you fear? How might God's providence help you face the imminent death of yourself or a loved one? Life is moving toward eternity and our glorification in God's way and time; we can trust him in it.

Faith in God's Providence Provides a Way to Discern His Will in Specific Situations

When asked to serve in our church or community, I wonder, *Should I say yes?* I can ask questions related to God's purposes: What decision will most glorify God? What resources has he given me for this situation? How will it make me more like Jesus? I have found God never asks me to do something when I think I am ready. I always think, *Maybe next year!* God wants me to depend on him, so he asks before I am confident in myself. Doing God's will involves faith on my part as God stretches me for my sanctification. The same is true for all his people. "And without faith it is impossible to please [God]" (Hebrews 11:6). Trusting God's providence means believing he knows what is ahead and will provide grace for the place (Proverbs 16:9). As I submit to God through prayer, he will make it clear. You may ask yourself these same questions when seeking God's will in specific situations you encounter.

Faith in God's Providence Produces Joy as I See Life Unfold under God's Direction

Being diagnosed with cancer was not "bad luck" or chance. Hard times became opportunities to grow in trusting God and seeing his goodness. My desire to be a mathematics teacher was also part of God's providence. The logical, orderly thought processes I learned have been invaluable in teaching the Bible and training teachers. Teaching mathematics was only for a season. Yet nothing is ever wasted in God's economy. What past experiences have prepared you for your current situation? How might God use them to help you know him in a deeper way?

Faith in God's Providence Strengthens Me for Criticism and Interruptions

Jesus loved his enemies and prayed for those who persecuted him. He asked God to forgive them as he was being nailed to the cross. I must do the same if I am to be like Jesus. Faith in his providence strengthens me for a Christlike attitude toward life even with criticism, interruptions, and oppression. I am to be kind and compassionate, forgiving others as God in Christ forgave me (Ephesians 4:32). I am to love them and pray for them. This calling is not unique to me; the same is true for every Christian.

God is not surprised by interruptions to my daily planner. He is sovereign over my time and may make up my lost time if I am able to return to my planned activities. However, it is up to God whether I ever resume my planned activities or whether he makes up my lost time in another way. He has something for me in each interruption that is for my good even though I may not see it in the moment. Everything is profitable toward my sanctification or the eternal good of others. Have you acknowledged that your time belongs to God and he is free to use it however he pleases? If you are in Christ, you belong to him, which means all you are and have are his, including the minutes of your day.

I am not to live according to the worldview set forth in music, TV, news, sitcoms, and movies. I am Christ's and I am to live in a way that embraces his purposes for me within his overarching plan of redeeming a people for himself. I am to be faithful to my calling in Christ. I am reminded of this each day when I read a small plaque on my wall I brought from the home of my aunt when she died. I had seen it there from my early childhood.

> Only one life,
> 'Twill soon be past,
> Only what's done
> For Christ will last.
> "For me to live is Christ."

What worldview determines your activities, pursuits, and pleasures? Does your worldview begin with God or does it begin with you? Which of your activities, pursuits, and pleasures would please God? Do they describe one who says, like Paul, "For me to live is Christ, and to die is gain" (Philippians 1:21)?

Faith in God's Providence Produces Hope in the Face of Disaster and Death

God has ordained the days laid out for each of us. Every day of our lives was planned before we were born (Psalm 139:16). The same truth is valid for our loved ones. My mother died at age fifty, two weeks after I was engaged to be married. I missed her presence as I planned and celebrated my wedding. Nevertheless, I was able to trust God's providence in the timing of her death. For Christians, the end of life on earth is merely the entrance into life in the presence of God.

God both lifts up and tears down for his glory and our eternal good (Lamentations 3:37–38). What comfort this brings when faced with a despotic ruler and potential persecution by terrorist groups! Knowing God is in control provides an antidote to the fear and frustration that characterize our culture. It also provides hope in the face of legislation that violates God's

Word. Are you comforted by God's providence as you read or listen to the world news?

My friends John and Debra believe God is sovereign over all things and that he is always good. They can quote Romans 8:28–29, "And we know that for those who love God all things work together for good, for those who are called according to his purpose. For those whom he foreknew he also predestined to be conformed to the image of his Son, in order that he might be the firstborn among many brothers." One day, Debra was called to put her faith into action.

I stopped and parked at a roadside rest stop on the way home from a drive with my three children—Marshall (5), Lucy (3), and Bowen (19 months). I remember parking in a parking spot, turning off the ignition, and walking around to the passenger side of our minivan to make a diaper change. After the diaper was on, I said, "It's time to buckle up; it's not safe to be on the side of the road when your seat belt is not buckled."

These next few events were all happening at the same time: Bowen was buckled up; Lucy, in the far rear passenger side, and Marshall, on the back driver's side, had not yet clicked their seat belts. My feet were on the ground while I reached to buckle Lucy. All of a sudden, I remember hearing a crash and feeling the van move as we were T-boned by a four-door pickup truck traveling 70 mph! I remember my shoes flying off and my legs feeling like flapping rag dolls. When the van stopped, I had been flung to the edge of the middle row looking toward the front of Bowen, who was still in his car seat. I could not find Lucy! I was unable to stand because of the laceration in my left leg, broken knee, and pretzel-like position of my legs. There was blood everywhere, the boys were screaming and crying, and I could not find Lucy! I kept calling out, "I have three children! Where is my daughter? God, you are still good, but where is my daughter?" I cried out over and over. I do not know how much time passed. It seemed to stand still.

The first responders were an off-duty fireman and a nurse. The fireman immediately put a tourniquet on my leg because there was so much blood everywhere. The nurse assured me she had called 911, and I gave her my husband's cell phone number, name, and place of employment. I kept repeating, "I have three children. I cannot find my daughter! I have three children. I cannot find my daughter!"

As the fireman finished tying a second tourniquet on my leg, the truck driver that hit us came around, hugged me, and said, "I'm so sorry! I'm so sorry!" I was in excruciating pain, and I remember saying, "Stop! Please stop hugging me! You're hurting me; my chest hurts!" I believe it was the nurse who walked him away from me toward the back end of the car.

Then Lucy stood up from under the front bumper of the man's truck, which was now inside our van, nearly touching the seat in which Bowen was still buckled! Lucy was crying hysterically but was alive! Glass was everywhere, and all three children were crying. I kept thanking God for saving our lives.

The ambulance staff and state trooper put the children on stretchers with neck braces in two different ambulances to go to the emergency room. Trusting the medics to take my two boys to the hospital—since I was strapped to a stretcher in a different ambulance—was the second hardest part of this event. Lucy was still very upset and crying. We were holding hands across the ambulance. I said, "Lucy, you like to sing. Can you sing us a song?" She began to sing "Jesus Loves Me" and stopped crying. Now the medics and I were crying. Mine were tears of joy.

Our precious pastor was waiting at the ER. His familiar face and calm, tender heart were just what the children needed. My husband arrived within moments.

This whole event has allowed powerful and meaningful conversations with my children. It has been an amazing lesson in trusting God's sovereignty, being thankful for his provision, and learning the depth of the word *forgiveness*. We forgive because he has forgiven us. Marshall, with tears in his eyes, asked, "But how do we forgive that man?" My reply to him was, "It's only the power of the Holy Spirit that allows us to do that! Without Christ, we would be in the same position as the man that was drunk behind the wheel and hit us. We would be sinning too."

Providentially, John and Debra had been teaching their children truth about God and were living it before this accident occurred. Lucy knew to sing about Jesus' love for her in this time of extreme chaos and confusion. They continued to trust God even in the midst of the agony of the moment. Their children saw them crying out to God and forgiving one who had caused them such trauma and pain. John and Debra were prepared to use this catastrophe as a platform to teach their children the gospel and to demonstrate forgiveness and trust in God's providence. Two years later, God continues to show his protective hand in their physical healing, financial settlements, and peace of mind.

What Next?

What will you do with the book of Esther? As you begin, read it several times to meet the characters and enjoy the story line. Get caught up in watching the drama unfold, lamenting over the villain, and cheering for God's people. Rejoice in the split-second timing that reveals God's providence without mentioning his name. Later lessons will focus on the details of the narrative. Read the words of the hymn each day and search for phrases that help you understand God's providence in the Scripture being studied.

Esther is not just the story of a woman who was used by God. It is the revelation of God's providence in the historical account of her life, her people, and all those in every age.

What truths about God's providence can you expect to find in this study?

- God's chief end is to display his glory. Our chief end is to glorify God and enjoy him forever. Glorifying God is not just worshiping him or doing what pleases him. It is being pleased with who God is and what God does. We cannot worship whom we do not enjoy. We cannot enjoy God if we are vying for his sovereign control over our lives.
- God has a plan and infallibly and sovereignly works to accomplish it. Where is your "free will" in this picture? Your will is free to do only what it desires. For all of us, our desires follow those of Adam and Eve in the garden until we are in Christ. In Christ, your desires are made new and your will is joyfully submitted to God's will (Philippians 2:13).
- His providence guarantees his purpose will happen as he planned.

- God ordains and controls each and every event. He is more than an observer; he is the initiator and governor. Does this mean that God ordains evil? Yes, it does. God is not evil, but he ordains it and uses evil people to accomplish his greater good, our holiness. It was God who sent Jesus to die on the cross to provide salvation for his sinful people (Acts 2:23). It was God who gave Paul a thorn in his flesh that he might prove God's grace was sufficient for his every need (2 Corinthians 12:9).
- God has a purpose and plan in everything that happens to each of us for his glory as well as our present welfare and eternal good.

Will you embrace these truths and strive to understand God's providence? Will you accept whatever God gives, believing he is sovereign over all events? This includes times of plenty and times of relatively less. It includes want and hardship. When we trust God's providence, we are at peace with it and enjoying it. Even more, we are at peace with God and enjoying God.

Closing Prayer

Gracious and providential God, you have provided the book of Esther at this time in my life. Surely this is no accident but one of the predetermined details in your plan and purpose for me. Please open my eyes to see your providence in the lives of each of the characters individually and collectively. Give me understanding of your providence in my life in the past, and help me see it in the days ahead. Then give me a heart to embrace your providence as it is—perfect, as you are. For your honor and glory. Amen.

Overview of Esther in God's Redemptive Plan

But seek the welfare of the city where I have sent you into exile, and pray to the LORD on its behalf, for in its welfare you will find your welfare. (Jeremiah 29:7)

Text

The book of Esther

Truth

God providentially weaves his plans for the world, the Jews, and individuals into his perfect plan of redemption.

Hymn: "God Moves in a Mysterious Way"

God moves in a mysterious way
His wonders to perform;
He plants his footsteps in the sea,
And rides upon the storm.

Deep in unfathomable mines
Of never-failing skill
He treasures up his bright designs,
And works his sovereign will.

Ye fearful saints, fresh courage take;
The clouds ye so much dread
Are big with mercy, and shall break
In blessings on your head.

Judge not the Lord by feeble sense,
But trust him for his grace;
Behind a frowning providence
He hides a smiling face.

His purposes will ripen fast,
Unfolding ev'ry hour;
The bud may have a bitter taste,
But sweet will be the flow'r.

Blind unbelief is sure to err,
And scan his work in vain;
God is his own interpreter,
And he will make it plain.

—WILLIAM COWPER, 1774

Opening Prayer

Lord God Almighty, I often forget that you are behind all that happens in our world and in our personal lives. Yet the

Bible reveals your providence in the rise and fall of nations, the deliverance of your people by unexpected means, and the daily affairs of people. Open my eyes to see your hand even when your name is not mentioned or your people seem more interested in the world than in you and your kingdom. Teach me through your mysterious ways to behold your wonders and to see them in my own life. For the glory of your name. Amen.

Questions for Study and Discussion

Overview of the Book of Esther

► SKIM THE BOOK OF ESTHER TO ENJOY THE STORY LINE AND MEET THE CHARACTERS

1. List the characters in the story and write one short fact about each that is new or interesting to you and why. Give the verse reference where you find your answer.

2. Where is God mentioned in the book?

3. Where do you see God's providence in the book?

4. Why do you think the author might have deliberately refrained from mentioning God, prayer, or worship in the book?

Reach of the Persian Empire

▶ REFER TO A MAP OF THE PERSIAN EMPIRE[1] AND LOCATE THESE PLACES MENTIONED IN THE BOOK OF ESTHER

1:1	127 provinces from India to Ethiopia
1:3	Persia, Media
1:5	Susa, the capital of Persia
2:6	Babylon

5. Compare the geographical size of the Persian Empire in Esther's day to your nation today.

6. How might the book of Esther have ended if Haman had succeeded in his evil plot?

1. If you are using an Internet search engine, type the phrase, "Map Persian Empire under Xerxes." *Xerxes* is his Greek name, *Ahasuerus* his Hebrew name.

7. How might the book of Esther help you in your present circumstances?

8. Write a prayer asking God to reveal himself in this study and to open your eyes to see him.

Commentary

Is there a God behind all that happens? Is there purpose in world and national affairs? Why are the Jews called "God's chosen people"? What is so special about them? How do they fit into the great plan of God's redemption? Who is Esther? How does she fit into God's plan? What is the Feast of Purim?

Where do you fit? Why has God chosen you to live at this time in history? in this place? in these circumstances? If you are a Christian, how does God want you to live? Perhaps you wonder what it means to be in the world but not of the world.

Let us set the stage for Esther's story and the answers to these questions. We will consider

- God's plan for the world, the Jews, and each individual;
- a brief overview of the history of the Jews;
- the characters in the book of Esther;
- the purpose of the book of Esther; and
- themes in the book of Esther.

God's Overarching Plan

God has an overarching plan for the world, for the Jews, and for each individual. His plan for each magnifies his power, his grace, his love for his people, and his holiness that demands justice. He providentially weaves them together to accomplish them all. What are these plans?

For the World: To Display His Glory (the Outshining of His Character)

God reveals his divine power and eternal nature in his

51

creation (Romans 1:20). He communicates his sovereignty, mercy, and grace by redeeming a people for himself through belief in his Son as Lord and Savior. He displays his holiness, righteousness, and justice through destruction of those who stand against him (Deuteronomy 7:9–10). Every individual is either with God by his grace alone through faith alone in Christ alone or is against God and his purposes. The Bible records the history of both groups of people and their relationship to God. In both cases, attention is called to God, the supreme and only sovereign.

For the Jews (Israel): To Reveal Him and His Plan to the Nations of the World

The Jews were set apart by God to be messengers of his truth and promised Messiah (Genesis 12:1–3; Romans 9:4–5). Throughout history, God's enemies have sought to thwart God's plan by destroying Israel through war, assimilation (Assyria, Persia), idolatry (Nebuchadnezzar), and eradication (Haman, Herod the Great, Hitler). The history of the Hebrew (Jewish) people is that they have survived as a people who are distinct from other cultures around them. They are unique among people groups in this regard. The *NIV Archaeological Study Bible* says,

> Throughout Israel's history God protected his chosen people from all kinds of dangers. Yes, he punished them when they refused to confess their sins and honor their covenant with him, but he was invariably also working behind the scenes, offering forgiveness and unfolding bigger plans for Israel and for all of humankind. During the reign of the Persian king Xerxes [also known as Ahasuerus] (486–465 B.C.) . . . God

used this powerful king and several obedient believers to save the Jews from extermination and to preserve the Davidic line through which the Messiah would descend.[2]

For Christians: To Be Ambassadors of the Lord Jesus Christ and to Be Like Him

God extended the blessing of being his ambassadors and messengers of reconciliation to all who believe in the Lord Jesus Christ as the Redeemer sent from God (2 Corinthians 5:18–20). God works to cause his redeemed to grow into the very likeness of Christ, reflecting his character (Romans 8:28–29; 2 Corinthians 3:18).

Brief Overview of the History of the Hebrew People (the Jews)

(Refer to your Bible's table of contents and a map of the Fertile Crescent.)

The history of mankind began in the Garden of Eden when God created Adam and Eve. After they sinned, the Old Testament history of the Hebrews can be traced through their journeys from Eden to Israel, out of Israel to Egypt, and back to Israel. Later, the Hebrews were called Jews. You might find it helpful to write these headings in the table of contents in your Bible.

Eden to Ur to Haran (Genesis 3:22–24; 11:9b, 31)

Adam and Eve sinned, so God sent them out of Eden and

---

2. "Introduction to Esther: Cultural Facts and Highlights," in *NIV Archaeological Study Bible: An Illustrated Walk Through Biblical History and Culture*, edited by Walter C. Kaiser Jr. and Duane Garrett (Grand Rapids: Zondervan, 2005), 714.

barred their return (Genesis 3). God dispersed the rebellious people at the Tower of Babel and confused their languages (Genesis 10–11; 11:9b). Some of the people went to Ur. Terah took his family from Ur to Haran, where they settled.

Haran to Israel (Genesis 12–45)

God called Terah's son Abram (later renamed Abraham) to be the father of the Hebrew nation. They were called to live by faith in God's promises and reveal his purposes to the world (Genesis 12). God promised to give them a land (Canaan) and to make Abraham's descendants as numerous as the stars in the sky and the sand on the seashore. Through Abraham's descendant (the Messiah, Jesus of Nazareth), the entire world would be blessed.

God's promise to Abraham was passed down to his son Isaac and Isaac's son Jacob (later renamed Israel), and then to Jacob's twelve sons. The tribes of the twelve sons of Jacob grew to be known as the nation of Israel. They are also called Hebrews. Judah, the fourth son of Jacob, would be the one through whom the promised Messiah would be born. Later, his descendants would be called Jews.

Israel to Egypt (Genesis 46–Exodus 12)

Jacob and his sons lived in the land of Canaan until God directed Jacob to take his family of 70 to Egypt during a famine (Genesis 46–50). They stayed there for 435 years until Moses led them out with a miraculous display of God's power against Pharaoh and the Egyptian gods (Exodus 1–12). The family had grown into a nation of 603,550 men from 20 years upward who were able to go to war (Numbers 1:45–46) plus the Levites, women, and children.

Egypt to Israel (Exodus 13–40; Leviticus; Numbers; Deuteronomy; Joshua)

The Israelites wandered in the desert for forty years because they did not trust God to lead them. They took possession of their Promised Land under Joshua but did not drive out everyone as God commanded.

Life in Israel

Life in Israel wasn't uniform in terms of leadership styles, the people's response to God, and so forth. Here is a quick overview of Israelite history once they reached the Promised Land:

Theocracy (God reigns) (Judges–1 Samuel 8). There was no appointed leader after Joshua died, so everyone did as he saw fit between periods in which Israel was ruled by judges. The period of the judges was defined by a cycle: The Israelites strayed from God. → They were overrun by a neighboring country. → They cried out to God for deliverance. → God sent a deliverer (judge). → They faithfully served God until the judge died and then returned to straying, starting the cycle anew.

United Kingdom (three kings reign in succession) (1 Samuel 9–2 Samuel 24; 1 Kings 1–11; 1 Chronicles 10–2 Chronicles 9). The people demanded a king like the other nations around them. God gave them Saul, David, and Solomon. Samuel anointed Saul and then David, thereby establishing the monarchy.

Divided Kingdom (two kings reign simultaneously, one in Israel and one in Judah) (1 Kings 12–2 Kings 25; 2 Chronicles 10–36). The kingdom was divided into two kingdoms with two kings upon the death of Solomon. Their history was characterized by increasing wandering from God and his purpose for them to glorify him.

- Israel (Northern Kingdom: nineteen kings, all ungodly)
- Judah (Southern Kingdom: twenty kings, only four godly and four a mixture of good and bad)[3]

Prophets called the people to return to the Lord their God to be blessed, and warned them of judgment and destruction if they refused (Isaiah, Jeremiah, Ezekiel, Hosea, Joel, Amos, Obadiah, Jonah, Micah, Nahum, Habakkuk, and Zephaniah). The prophets also pointed people to the coming of the promised Messiah.

The Exile of Israel to Assyria and Judah to Babylon (2 Kings 17:6–18; 25; 2 Chronicles 36:15–21). Sadly, the people ignored the prophets. The result was the exile of Israel (Northern Kingdom, ten tribes) to the nation of Assyria and the exile of Judah (Southern Kingdom, two tribes) to Babylon. The recorded history of the Northern Kingdom ends with this exile. The exile of Judah occurred in three stages as did Judah's return at the end of seventy years. Details of the three stages of the exile may be found in the historical accounts of 2 Chronicles, Ezra, Nehemiah, Esther, Jeremiah, Daniel, and in Lamentations, the anonymous poetic account of the fall of Jerusalem. King Nebuchadnezzar of Babylon also carried away treasures from the temple and king's palace in Jerusalem.

The following dates are a compilation of timelines from the *NIV Archaeological Study Bible: Introductions to Ezra, Nehemiah,*

3. "Evaluating Kings of Israel and Judah in 1–2 Kings," under 1 Kings 15 in the *ESV® Study Bible* (Wheaton, IL: Crossway, 2008).

Esther, and Daniel along with deduced dates from putting together the events in Esther. Some scholars give slightly different dates, but these are included for your understanding of the high points of the historical setting for the book of Esther. For details of these events, read the Scriptures listed in the paragraph above.

605–536 BC (70 years)	Daniel's time in Babylon
605 BC	First exiles, including Daniel and his three friends, and first looting of temple
586 BC	Fall of Jerusalem: walls demolished and temple destroyed
539 BC	Daniel sent to the lions' den and afterward raised to a position of power in Babylon
539 BC	Persian King Cyrus conquers Babylonian empire, including Israel and Judah

Fig. 2.1. Timeline for the Life of Daniel

Babylon to Jerusalem (three stages recorded in Ezra, Nehemiah, Haggai, and Zechariah). The return of the exiles from Babylon to Jerusalem began with a decree issued by Cyrus declaring that Jewish exiles throughout the empire were free to return to their ancestral home (2 Chronicles 36:22–23). As in their exile, the return to Jerusalem was in stages. The first group to return rebuilt the temple and city under the leadership of Zerubbabel and the priest Jeshua (Ezra 1–6). The second group returned with Ezra eighty years after the first (Ezra 7–10). Ezra had several tasks: he was responsible for reading and teaching the law to the people (Ezra 7:10, 25–26) and was charged by Persian authorities to return gifts for the temple (7:14–20). Under Nehemiah's leadership, the third group of returning exiles rebuilt the city walls in fifty-two days despite difficulties (Nehemiah 6:15) and recommitted to fulfill covenant obligations. Ezra visited Jerusalem again eight years after his first visit. His reading of the Law and covenant-renewal ceremony were part of the joyous dedication of the completed wall.

538 BC	Cyrus's decree
537–515 BC	First return of exiles
536 BC	End of Daniel's ministry
486–465 BC	Reign of Ahasuerus (Xerxes) over the Persian Empire (100 years after fall of Jerusalem and 50 years after Daniel)
483 BC	Ahasuerus's banquets (third year of his reign)
479 BC	Esther crowned queen in Persia (seventh year of Ahasuerus)
458 BC	Second return of exiles
445 BC	Third return of exiles
433–423 BC	Ezra's return visit
c. 460–350 BC	Book of Esther written

Fig. 2.2. Esther's Relationship to Returning Exiles

Why did everyone not go at once? God providentially and sovereignly called the ones he entrusted with the task of rebuilding. "Then rose up the heads of the fathers' houses of Judah and Benjamin, and the priests and the Levites, *everyone whose spirit God had stirred to go* up to rebuild the house of the LORD that is in Jerusalem" (Ezra 1:5). The story of Esther is about some who remained in Persia. Can you imagine the chaos if all had returned at once to the city that was only rubble?

Within this historical setting, let us turn our attention to the book of Esther and the people whose lives are portrayed in it.

The Cast of Characters

King Ahasuerus is a powerful king of the huge Persian Empire. He displays his power and wealth in an ostentatious manner. He makes rash decisions at times, but calls on his counselors at other times. His edicts are for the entire Persian Empire; they cannot be revoked once they are sealed with his signet ring.

Queen Vashti loses favor with the king by refusing to be displayed before the men at his banquet. She loses her crown, making way for a successor who fits in with God's plans for his exiled people.

Esther is the heroine, and her character is masterfully developed in the compelling narrative. Did you find it difficult to put down? Did you wish it had more chapters? Did your attitude toward Esther change as the plot developed? Esther is a Jewish orphan in Persia who never lived in the Promised Land. She first appears in her story as a compliant young woman who wins a beauty contest to determine the next Persian queen. She seems quite comfortable in the harem of the pagan king. No one there even knows she is a Jew. As the narrative unfolds, it becomes increasingly clear that she is hidden away in exile in Persia for God's purpose. After ten years, God brings her to the forefront to work out his plan for the Jews and for her. She is asked to risk her life to save her people, and she does.

Mordecai, also a Jew, is Esther's cousin and guardian. He becomes another key person in saving the Jews by exposing a plot to kill the king. Later he is exalted to the position second to the king.

Haman, the villain, is promoted to power by the king. Out of anger toward Mordecai he plots a way to destroy all the Jews in the empire. God providentially turns the plan upside down and uses Haman's own efforts to destroy him.

Other characters include Zeresh, Haman's wife, and the king's advisors—Hegai, the eunuch in charge of the harem, and Hathach, the eunuch messenger between Esther and Mordecai.

The Purpose of the Book

Encouragement

While Esther lived in Persia, the Jews who had returned to Jerusalem faced tremendous opposition. Surrounding nations did everything in their power to discourage the returned exiles from rebuilding Jerusalem and restoring the temple worship that distinguished them from other nations. At one point, they stopped work for sixteen years. Esther may have been written for their encouragement. They would need a reminder that God providentially works to preserve his people in the face of diabolic opposition.

Explanation of Purim

The Jews in future generations might also have asked, "Why do we celebrate the Feast of Purim? It is not mentioned in the Law of Moses." The book of Esther answers this question.

Reminder of God's Sovereignty

In every generation, we need the reminder that God is sovereign and providentially protects his people. His purposes cannot be thwarted by opponents or by the worldliness of his people.

Themes in Esther

God's Providence

God sovereignly works through people, circumstances, split-second timing, and previously established laws and rulers to accomplish his predetermined plan for the Jews, individuals, and the world.

The Lure of the World to Assimilate God's People

Throughout history, God's people have been attracted to the world system that marginalizes, ignores, or replaces God with idols. God has called his people to be distinct from those around them so that they can be his messengers of the gospel to a lost and dying world.

Life in a Pagan World

In the face of temptation and persecution, it would be natural for the Jews to despair. The stability of familiar temple worship was not possible. What would be their foundation? How should they relate to the emperor, his officials, and the people yet maintain their distinction as God's chosen people?

God's Deliverance of His People

God protected a remnant of the nation of Israel who returned to Jerusalem. He also protected the Jews who remained in Persia. For them, there was no miraculous parting of the Red Sea

(Exodus 14) or pushing back of the Jordan River (Joshua 3). Yet God's hand is evident as he used his people in their pagan environment. There is no mention of prayer, sacrifices, or offerings in the book of Esther, but God's providential deliverance of his people cannot be missed. God's faithfulness does not depend on our faithfulness.

God's Use of Unlikely People

Mordecai and Esther were ordinary people living in exile when God began to turn their world upside down with the removal of Vashti, preparing the place for Esther to serve him and her people. The returned exiles must have been encouraged to hear about Mordecai and Esther. Even in a setting like Susa, God used his people to preserve his chosen nation and their part in his plan of redemption.

God's Power That Turns Persecution onto the Persecutors

God's people may be put in life-threatening situations or suffer persecution. However, those who think they can destroy God's people and plan find they are fighting against God. God will ultimately use the plans of the persecutors for their own destruction, though not always in this life.

What about Your Life?

Why has God allowed you to live at this time in history? in this place? in these circumstances? The apostle Paul wrote that God has set the period of time and the place where you live that you might seek him (Acts 17:26–27). How have you experienced attempts by yourself or others to thwart God's purposes for your holiness, Christlikeness, and gospel witness? Where are you tempted by the lure of the world to assimilate into its mold of self-indulgence, self-reliance, complaining, blaming, indulging, and so on? How are you living for Christ in a pagan environment? Have you seen God's power providentially turn persecution onto those who persecute you and others? What difference does your life make in God's great plan of redemption?

Perhaps you have asked, "You want me to do what? Why me, Lord? This is too hard—no, it is impossible!" You may be waiting for God to bring someone forward in your difficulty while God's purpose is to bring you forward for the sake of others. You may not have yet seen God's hand at work, but that does not mean he is not working. Embracing God's providence in your life will bless you and open your eyes to see truth about God you never imagined. God moves in mysterious ways his wonders to perform.

More than once I have asked God, *"You want me to do what?"* He has faithfully confirmed his call to me as I have accepted the call and trusted his providence.

I was called to teach a Bible Study Fellowship (BSF) class. The thought was overwhelming. My children were four and six years old. I was managing a household on a tight budget. Where would I find the time? Did I really have enough knowledge to take on such a responsibility? As I listened to the current teaching leader, I asked myself, "What if I refuse this opportunity?" I immediately thought, "Then God will give the privilege and joy to another; and I will sit here week after week watching how he blesses her with what he is offering me." I knew that God was giving me a privilege I must not refuse, even though the corresponding responsibility was huge and the task seemed impossible. My husband encouraged me to rise up to the challenge. My pastor did as well. My understanding of the responsibility and privilege grew as I stepped forward in faith. Both grew exponentially as I trusted God and experienced his loving concern and mighty power on my behalf.

Closing Prayer

Providential, all-wise, ever-present God, teach me what it means to live for you and your glory. May I grow to be a loyal, courageous, and faithful servant of you and the Lord Jesus Christ. May I be more concerned with the eternal destiny of others than with my own comfort, reputation, and life. Open my eyes to see your providence in my life. Let me embrace your providence day by day as you mold me into the likeness of Christ, empower me to serve you, and prepare me for heaven. For the glory of your name. Amen.

Setting the Stage for Esther

Vashti is never again to come before King Ahasuerus. And let the king give her royal position to another who is better than she. (Esther 1:19)

Text

Esther 1

Truth

God knows the future and providentially orders current events to accomplish his purposes.

Hymn: "O Father, You Are Sovereign"[1]

O Father, you are sovereign
In all the worlds you made;

---

1. © Margaret Clarkson, "O Father, You Are Sovereign" (Carol Stream, IL: Hope Publishing Company, 1982). All rights reserved. Used by permission.

Your mighty word was spoken
And light and life obeyed.
Your voice commands the seasons
And bounds the ocean's shore,
Sets stars within their courses
And stills the tempest's roar.

O Father, you are sovereign
In all affairs of man;
No pow'rs of death or darkness
Can thwart your perfect plan.
All chance and change transcending,
Supreme in time and space,
You hold your trusting children
Secure in your embrace.

O Father, you are sovereign,
The Lord of human pain,
Transmuting earthly sorrows
To gold of heav'nly gain.
All evil overruling,
As none but Conqu'ror could,
Your love pursues its purpose—
Our souls' eternal good.

O Father, you are sovereign!
We see you dimly now,
But soon before your triumph
Earth's every knee shall bow.
With this glad hope before us
Our faith springs up anew:

our sovereign Lord and Savior,
we trust and worship you!

—MARGARET CLARKSON, 1982

Opening Prayer

Lord God Almighty, you are Providence. How comforting to know that you know the future and powerfully work to accomplish your purposes for your people. Open my eyes to see your providence in the book of Esther and also in my own life. May I begin to see your love pursuing your purpose for me. With glad hope for the present and the future, increase my faith each day and fill my heart with worship of you, O sovereign Lord and Savior. For your glory and my eternal good. Amen.

Questions for Study and Discussion

Three Royal Feasts

▶ READ ESTHER 1:1–9

1. Describe the three feasts mentioned: Who is present? Why do they take place? Where are they located? How long do they last?
   a. First feast (vv. 1–4)

b. Second feast (vv. 5–8)

c. Third feast (v. 9)

2. What are some words you might use to describe the garden court in the king's palace?

3. Define *arrogance*, *opulence*, and *wealth*. How are they similar and how are they different? Give a current example of each that illustrates their relationship.

The King's Problem

▶ READ ESTHER 1:10–12

4. What was the king's order, and what might have been his motive in it?

5. Why do you think the men who served in the king's presence were eunuchs?

6. How did the queen surprise the king, and what was his response?

The Charge against the Queen

▶ READ ESTHER 1:13–20

7. To whom did the king turn to resolve this dilemma?

8. To whom do you turn first to resolve your problems? Give an example supporting your answer.

9. What was the charge against the queen for refusing the king's command? Who made the charge?

10. What motivated their charge?

11. What did they counsel the king to do? Why?

The Counselors' Advice

▶ READ ESTHER 1:21–22

12. How did the king respond to the advice of his counselors?

13. Why do you think the wise men emphasized that every man should "be master in his own household" (v. 22)?

14. What principles for your life can you discern from the action of the king and his counselors?

15. How might you use these principles this week?

Two Kings

▶ REVIEW ESTHER 1

16. What decisions are you facing today, and what are the temporal, long-range, and eternal consequences of the options before you? How will you avoid making a choice based on fear, anger, or pride?

17. How would you compare King Ahasuerus and his kingdom with Christ and his kingdom?

18. How does this help you relate to Christ as King and Lord?

Commentary

Many people spend much time, effort, money, and emotions trying to determine what the future holds. They start their day with a cup of coffee and their horoscope. Predictions abound following a natural disaster or during a political campaign. In the face of a crisis, some turn to fortunetellers to find a lost child or solve other needs. Others shake their fist at God, enraged by what he did to cause or did not do to prevent their suffering and shame. Sadly, they miss what God has done to bear their suffering and shame through his Son.

God does not deal with us according to our faithfulness but according to his. In Esther's day, God protected Jews who had returned to their homeland. God also protected Jews who remained in Persia. God's purposes stood because of God, not because of them. Yet he providentially worked and used his people to accomplish his purpose for them. The same is true for his people in all ages.

While God's name is not mentioned in the book of Esther, he is the real hero of the book. His providence shines through the details of the compelling narrative as it unfolds. He providentially removed Vashti to make room for Esther to be queen. As queen, Esther would be able to help her people.

The King and His Kingdom (1:1–2)

"In the days of Ahasuerus" describes the time between chapters 6 and 7 of the book of Ezra (486–465 BC). Ahasuerus is also known by his Greek name, Xerxes. Gaebelein says that secular historians and ancient inscriptions portray Ahasuerus as opulent, extravagant, and irrational.[2] The writer of Esther certainly agrees.

The *NIV Archaeological Study Bible* explains that Ahasuerus was living in the Persian winter capital, Susa, one of four capital cities of Persia.[3] It was customary for kings to be attended by eunuchs, who would be unable to build their own kingdom or dynasty or start an uprising. The king's large harem was also attended by eunuchs who were responsible to protect the king's "property."

Ahasuerus's kingdom, the Persian Empire, occupied one-half of the then-known world, including present-day Iran. The area included 127 provinces from India (present-day Pakistan) to Ethiopia (present-day Sudan).[4] The Jews who had not chosen to return to their land under the former King Cyrus were dispersed throughout the Persian Empire. Haman's edict covered all of that territory (3:8).

The *NIV Archaeological Study Bible* records the rout of the massive army of Darius, the father of Ahasuerus, by the Greeks at the battle of Marathon in 490 BC. Following Darius's death in 486 BC, Ahasuerus succeeded him as king.[5] "After taking the throne he first had to deal with rebellions in Egypt and Babylon, but he soon turned his attention to Greece. Planning a new invasion, he put together perhaps the largest army of ancient history and . . . built up a formidable navy."[6]

---

2. Frank E. Gaebelein, ed., *1 & 2 Kings, 1 & 2 Chronicles, Ezra, Nehemiah, Esther, Job*, The Expositor's Bible Commentary, vol. 4 (Grand Rapids: Zondervan, 1988), 789.

3. Study note on Esther 1:2 in the *NIV Archaeological Study Bible* (Grand Rapids: Zondervan, 2005).

4. Study note on Esther 1:1 in the *ESV*® *Study Bible* (Wheaton, IL: Crossway, 2008).

5. *NIV Archaeological Study Bible*, 717.

6. Ibid., 718.

The Splendor of the King's Court (1:3–9)

The king displayed his wealth and splendor with two extravagant feasts. The first feast, for military leaders, princes, and nobles from all provinces—the elite of his kingdom—in the third year of his reign, lasted 180 days. Showing the riches of his glorious kingdom included displaying at the feast items taken out of his royal treasure house. The sacred vessels brought from the Jerusalem temple under Nebuchadnezzar would likely have been shown. The *NIV Archaeological Study Bible* says, "The Greek historian Herodotus explained that the Persians drank as they deliberated matters of state, believing that intoxication put them in closer touch with the spiritual world."[7] Probably this feast corresponded with Ahasuerus's plans to invade Greece.

At the end of the 180 days of feasting and planning, the king gave a second feast lasting seven days for all the people in Susa, both nobles and commoners. It was held in the court of the garden of the king's palace. The *Expositor's Bible Commentary* says, "Archaeologists have found the remains of Xerxes' palace and have verified the accuracy of the opulence described in this verse [1:6]."[8] The detailed description of the curtains, hangings, furniture, pillars, mosaic pavement, drinking vessels, and so on. reveals the opulent, extravagant, grandiose lifestyle of the king. He wanted to gain the support of his people by impressing them with his wealth and splendor. "The royal wine was lavished according to the bounty of the king" (1:7b) and according to the desire of each man. Each drank as much or as little as he wanted and when he wanted.

7. Ibid. study note on Esther 1:10–12.
8. Gaebelein, *Esther*, Expositor's Bible Commentary, 799.

While the king entertained the men, Queen Vashti held a third feast for the women in the palace. "Separate banquets were not unusual in that culture."[9] Neither were they required.[10]

Truth: Arrogance and Opulence Go Hand in Hand

Opulence—ostentatious, extravagant excess; lavish and visibly over-the-top living—goes hand in hand with pride. The more you have, the more you may be tempted to display your abundance, prosperity, and riches to impress others and win their favor. Pride is at the head of the list of things the Lord despises (Proverbs 6:16–19).

What is your motive in inviting others to your home? Is it sharing your possessions or showing them off? Wealth is not evil, but misuse of wealth is. God entrusts some with great wealth that they may use it to advance his kingdom and help his people. Do you know people like that? Are you one of them? How are you using what God has entrusted to you? (See Matthew 25:14–30; 2 Corinthians 8–9.)

The End of Vashti (1:10–22)

On the seventh and final day of the feast, the king was merry with wine. He ordered his seven eunuchs to bring Queen Vashti before him with her royal crown. He wanted to display her beauty to his guests. Gaebelein writes, "Some Jewish sources interpreted the order to mean that she was to appear nude, except for her crown."[11] It seems that she was just another piece of the king's property.

9. John F. Walvoord and Roy B. Zuck, eds., *The Bible Knowledge Commentary: Old Testament* (Wheaton, IL: Victor Books, 1985), 702.
10. Gaebelein, *Esther*, Expositor's Bible Commentary, 799.
11. Ibid., 800.

But the queen refused. What a turn of events! The king was publicly humiliated, losing face with potential allies for his Greek conquest and also with his own people. He could display his wealth for 180 days and hold a lavish feast for 7 days, but he could not control his wife. This enraged the king and his anger burned within him.

This was no small dilemma. What should he do? He looked to his closest official advisors, seven men who were well versed in law and judgment and were trained to advise the king so he could maintain power and prestige (Esther 1:13; see also Ezra 7:14). They had special access to the king, for they "saw the king's face, and sat first in the kingdom" (Esther 1:14). He posed the question, "According to the law, what is to be done to Queen Vashti, because she has not performed the command of King Ahasuerus delivered by the eunuchs?" (1:15).

The advisors wasted no time in their deliberation. The charge against the queen was all-inclusive. She had done wrong against the king, against all the officials, and against all the peoples in all the king's provinces. But actually, their charge stretched the truth; she had only disobeyed the king. What was the reasoning behind this charge? They feared that all the women would hear about what the queen did and her example would cause them to look at their husbands with contempt. This breakdown of order in the home could spread throughout the kingdom. Of special interest to the seven counselors were probably the noble women, their wives, who would show contempt and wrath for the officials—them.

The enormity of the charge required a corresponding recommendation. The king should send a royal order that could not be repealed. Vashti was never again to come before King Ahasuerus. Furthermore, the king would give her royal position to another who was better than she (one who would comply with the king's wishes). Her punishment fit her crime. She refused to come to the king, so now she was forbidden to do so. She would serve as an example of what happens to women who do not honor their husbands. These advisors expected that all women, high and low, would give honor to their husbands because of the decree. How foolish to believe that they could legislate genuine submission, obedience, and respect.

It is not surprising that their advice pleased the king. Every man was to be master in his own household. If other wives followed the queen's example, they should receive the same sentence. Letters were immediately dispatched to "all the royal provinces, to every province in its own script and to every people in its own language" (1:22). Did you notice the special care that was taken to make sure that every man and woman heard and understood this decree? This was no small matter considering the size of the empire.

Truth: God Providentially Uses the Sinful, Foolish Ways of People for His Own Purposes

The king was enraged at the queen's behavior. He and the other men feared that the men in the kingdom would lose their power over their wives. Rage and fear led them to the foolish decision and edict. How ironic that his edict guaranteed what he feared—his impotence at home would spread by requiring everyone to hear of it. Rage and fear were not good motives for making wise decisions or gaining respect. But God used them for his purpose of protecting his people. Vashti's dismissal was Esther's opening.

Where are you tempted to make decisions based on impulse, fear, or anger? Beware of yielding to that temptation, "for God gave us a spirit not of fear but of power and love and self-control" (2 Timothy 1:7). What is your response when faced with a dilemma? To whom do you go first for advice? Our King,

Jesus, is always good, wise, and all-powerful. Will you go first to him, believing that he will direct you in his good and perfect way?

> Trust in the LORD with all your heart,
>   and do not lean on your own understanding.
> In all your ways acknowledge him,
>   and he will make straight your paths. (Proverbs 3:5–6)

> If any of you lacks wisdom, let him ask God, who gives generously to all without reproach, and it will be given him. But let him ask in faith, with no doubting. (James 1:5–6a)

Time Lapse: Invasion of Greece

"After these things" (Esther 2:1) describes a time lapse from Vashti's removal in the third year of Ahasuerus's reign (1:3) to Esther's crowning in the seventh year (2:16). Gaebelein explains that Ahasuerus's attention had returned to the Greek war and amassing his immense army and formidable naval fleet. Alas! He retreated home in defeat in 479 BC.[12] By now his anger toward Vashti had abated, and he remembered her. However, she was no longer his queen due to his rage and fear, and the counsel of his advisors. There was no turning back; his edict was irrevocable. It is even possible that she had been executed.

Truth: Some Choices Have Irreversible Consequences in God's Irrevocable Plan

It is impossible to take back words spoken in rage that wound the spirit of a child or spouse. It is impossible to offer yourself as a

12. Ibid., 804.

virgin to your spouse if you have given yourself to another before your marriage. The gift of salvation that God has provided through Jesus Christ is for this life; there are no opportunities after death.

> And just as it is appointed for man to die once, and after that comes judgment, so Christ, having been offered once to bear the sins of many, will appear a second time, not to deal with sin but to save those who are eagerly waiting for him. (Hebrews 9:27–28)

Perhaps you are living with the irreversible consequences of your own choices. Is there hope for you? There is hope for those in Christ. God can use even those difficult consequences for his good purposes in your life (Romans 8:28–29). What choices are you facing today? Before you make an important decision, what can you do to discern the long-range, temporal, and eternal consequences of your choices? Will you avoid making a choice based on fear, anger, or pride?

The most important decision anyone makes is to run to God for the salvation he has provided through his Son, the Lord Jesus Christ. If you have received this gift from God, you may run to the loving arms of your heavenly Father moment by moment so that he may direct your paths. He may not reverse the consequences of your foolish choices, but he will give you full forgiveness and the grace to live through them while he uses them for your sanctification.

Truth: Some Choices Have Unforeseen Blessings in God's Irrevocable Plan

It was a normal Saturday afternoon on Memorial Day Weekend 2015. Allen and Becca were planning a trip with their two young sons to their family's weekend getaway in Wimberley, Texas. They had invited friends for barbecue and swimming in the Blanco River. By God's providence, Allen decided to wait until the next morning to go.

Allen's parents, Brenda and H.C., clearly saw God's providential hand protecting their loved ones. In the middle of the night, rain fell in such huge amounts that the river rose more than forty feet in three hours, moving their cabin from its foundation. A broken glass door allowed the house to fill with seven feet of water, keeping it from floating down the river. Had they been there, it is unlikely they would have heard the roar of the water in time to run up the steep drive to safety. Their car would have been swept away by the powerful water that took their neighbor's car. God providentially stopped their plans to spend the night there.

My friends saw God's loving care of them in other ways. While they lost many things, some cherished items were amazingly protected. Photo books of my family's weekends with them and a watercolor of the Blanco River from my granddaughter, Gracie, were still dry in a Ziploc plastic bag on top of a table. Oil paintings by H.C.'s mother were salvaged; Brenda's father's swing is still hanging from a tree waiting for someone to sit in it and enjoy the view of the river. Only God's loving hand could have kept those items intact.

Allen's choice to wait until the next morning brought this family unforeseen blessings. Their entire family has a greater understanding of God's loving hand of protection and a deeper realization that God guides them even when they are not actively seeking his will. They lived through the 2015 Texas floods with growing trust in God's providence—a new household term.

Who knows what the future holds for you as well as your family, church, community, and nation? Who knows what choices you will face and what their consequences will be? There is only one who does—the Lord God Almighty. Because he knows your past and future, he providentially works in the present to accomplish his temporal and eternal purposes for you and for his kingdom. His presence may not be obvious and his work may seem slow, but he is working to accomplish his purpose for you. Will you trust him and look for his providence in your life today as he prepares you for tomorrow and for eternity? He may be preparing you to play a significant role in the salvation of others. He does not deal with us according to our faithfulness but according to his.

The world of Susa was much like our world today. In many places, the reins of power are in the hands of incompetent, amoral, or immoral people. Often there is a dangerous disconnect between wisdom and power. Sadly, this is also true in the homes of Christian people. Husbands "lead" their wives by authoritative suppression rather than Christlike, sacrificial love that generates godly submission (Ephesians 5:25–33). If you are a woman in that situation, God has a word for you as well: "Likewise, wives, be subject to your own husbands, so that even if some do not obey the word, they may be won without a word by the conduct of their wives, when they see your respectful and pure conduct" (1 Peter 3:1–2). Parents who fear the loss of their children's respect administer harsh rules in rage with no evidence of loving discipline and grace that trains children to welcome God's discipline as good (Hebrews 12:5–11). Offering love, kindness, and grace paves the way for true appreciation, while demanding obedience produces resentment and erects barriers. You cannot legislate love or respect; they are earned or given as a gift of God's grace.

Although God is not mentioned in Esther 1, he was providentially working behind the scenes to accomplish what was ahead. The irrevocable law of Ahasuerus was right in line with God's plan for two Jewish people in Persia—Esther and Mordecai.

Our God and his kingdom are different from Ahasuerus and his kingdom. God works quietly behind the scenes with wisdom, power, and purpose. Ahasuerus reacted with fear and an unwise knee-jerk display of his authority. God's law flows from his unchanging goodness and power. Ahasuerus's law flowed from his narcissism and fear of losing power. God demonstrated his love for his people and his glory (John 3:16); Ahasuerus demonstrated his love for himself and his comfort. The holy kingdom of God and the worldly kingdom of Ahasuerus—and earthly kingdoms of our own day—have different goals and means to accomplish those goals.

Which kingdom and its principles have your allegiance? God has already demonstrated his love for you in Christ (1 John 4:9–10). Warfare and calamity may face the followers of Jesus Christ, but we are promised,

> Though we walk in the flesh, we are not waging war according to the flesh. For the weapons of our warfare are not of the flesh but have divine power to destroy strongholds. We destroy arguments and every lofty opinion raised against the knowledge of God, and take every thought captive to obey Christ. (2 Corinthians 10:3–5)

Why? Most of us ask that question at some point in our lives. God's providence is good, but it is not always easy. Why does God take a thirty-four-year-old man after a year of painful cancer treatment and let a ninety-five-year-old linger with mind, ears, and eyes that have failed? Why did some people die in the terrorist attack on September 11, 2001, and others live? Why does God not stop the execution of Christians by terrorists? It is unwise to try to answer these questions. A better question is, *Who?* Who is it that controls the events of history for his purposes? What are his purposes? What is he like? Can I trust him? He is God Almighty who is all-wise, all-knowing, and perfect love. He has already demonstrated his love in providing the Lord Jesus Christ to be the substitutionary atonement for our sins. We can trust him.

Closing Prayer

O great, providential God, it is frightening to think that my life is in the hands of sinful, arrogant people who care nothing about you or about me. Guard me from the dangers of pride, opulence, fear, rage, and anger. Help me train my mind to think of you, not others, as the sovereign Lord who is bringing your plan for me to your predetermined end one step at a time. As I face choices, give me wisdom to look ahead to the consequences and to choose wisely in line with your purposes. Thank you for your grace and mercy to me each day. In the name of Jesus I pray. Amen.

The New Queen: Esther

He set the royal crown on her head and made her
queen. (Esther 2:17)

Text

Esther 2

Truth

God providentially prepares his people and circumstances
to accomplish his purposes.

Hymn: "Whate'er My God Ordains Is Right"

Whate'er my God ordains is right:
His holy will abideth;
I will be still whate'er he doth,
And follow where he guideth.
He is my God; though dark my road,
He holds me that I shall not fall:
Wherefore to him I leave it all.

Whate'er my God ordains is right:
He never will deceive me;
He leads me by the proper path;
I know he will not leave me.
I take, content, what he hath sent;
His hand can turn my griefs away,
And patiently I wait his day.

Whate'er my God ordains is right:
Though now this cup, in drinking,
May bitter seem to my faint heart,
I take it, all unshrinking.
My God is true; each morn anew
Sweet comfort yet shall fill my heart,
And pain and sorrow shall depart.

Whate'er my God ordains is right:
Here shall my stand be taken;
Though sorrow, need, or death be mine,
Yet am I not forsaken.
My Father's care is round me there;
He holds me that I shall not fall:
And so to him I leave it all.

—SAMUEL RODIGAST, 1675

Opening Prayer

Sovereign Creator God, you are the one true God who alone knows the future and provides all that is needed to accomplish your purposes. I acknowledge you do not need me but are pleased to allow me to approach you with adoration, thanksgiving, confession, and petitions for others and myself. I need you and your Word to show me your will that I may walk in it with confidence. Teach me through this lesson to trust you more fully and love you more dearly, confident that whatever you ordain is right and your holy will abides. For the glory of your name and your Son. Amen.

Questions for Study and Discussion

1. What words or phrases from the hymn "Whate'er My God Ordains Is Right" did you find helpful for your life today?

2. How does this hymn help you to understand God's providence?

Wanted: New Queen

▶ READ ESTHER 2:1–4

3. Explain the plan for a new queen proposed by the king's young attendants. Do you think it was reasonable? Why or why not?

4. What qualities would the candidate for queen need to please the king? (See also chapter 1.)

5. Would you have liked yourself, your daughter, or your sister to be a candidate for queen? Give reasons for your answer.

A Dispersed People

► READ ESTHER 2:5–7

6. Should Mordecai and Esther have been in Susa instead of their homeland? See 2 Chronicles 36:17–21 and Ezra 1.

Esther Finds Favor

▶ READ ESTHER 2:7–11

7. Why do you think Esther, a Jew, was chosen to be among the candidates for queen?

8. Do you think she had the option to refuse to be a candidate? Give biblical reasons for your answer. (See also Genesis 41:37–57; Daniel 1:1–21.)

9. What about Esther pleased the harem chief, Hegai, and how did he show favor to her?

10. Why might Mordecai have been concerned that Esther not reveal her Jewish heritage?

11. Was it right for Esther to conceal her heritage? Give reasons for your answer.

Preparing to Please the King

▶ READ ESTHER 2:12–18

12. What did Esther have to do to prepare for her time with the king?

13. What was the result of Esther's preparation and response to the favor of Hegai?

14. What do you learn from Esther about relating to those in authority over you?

Influence: A Mixed Blessing

▶ READ ESTHER 2:19–23

15. How did Esther and Mordecai gain influence with the king?

16. How might their worldly advantage be potentially disastrous spiritually? How might it be potentially useful spiritually?

17. How might your worldly advantage be potentially dangerous to your spiritual life? How might it be potentially useful?

18. What might be *God's* purpose for giving it to you?

Found: God's Providence

▶ REVIEW ESTHER 2:1–23

19. Where do you see God's providence in this chapter?

20. How have you seen God's providence overrule to save and prepare you to serve him?

21. Write a prayer of thanksgiving to God for his providence in your life. Include any phrases from "Whate'er My God Ordains Is Right" that reflect your gratitude.

Commentary

Do current events alarm you or cause you anxiety and fear? Why does God allow evil to continue and even escalate? Where is he, and what is the answer to the decline of our culture? One of the most encouraging truths about God is that he, as sovereign Creator and ruler, exercises his power to guide history and sustain human destiny. God himself is the answer for every people group. He knows the future and calls individuals to accomplish his purposes for them and for the world. He uses his imperfect people and even pagan rulers to deliver his disobedient or immature people. He cares for his people wherever they are. He will bring them to the finish line.

God's providence in Persia becomes clearer through the events of Esther 2. The evidence of his favor toward Esther and Mordecai is progressively seen. He prepares them through the search for a new Persian queen to be in the place of influence to protect his people when they would later be threatened by annihilation. God wrote the script for their lives as he does for all individuals. He providentially prepares his people to accomplish his preordained purposes.

The Search for a New Queen (Esther 2:1–4)

Returning from his failure to conquer Greece, King Ahasuerus remembered his beautiful Queen Vashti, but she was no longer able to enter his presence, whether by his own irrevocable decree or by her death. His young attendants—personal servants who were different from the wise legal advisors—discerned his unhappiness, so they came to his aid with a plan. He needed another queen better than Vashti (1:19). Surely she must be at least as beautiful as Vashti, but she must also be one who would please him by complying with his every command. Their plan included four stages.

Stage One: Search

First, they would conduct a nationwide search in all the provinces to select candidates for his queen. The candidates had to be beautiful, young, and virgins (unmarried). This was not a position a young woman would seek but one for which she was drafted. Parents did not bring their daughters; the king appointed officials to search for and gather the candidates.

Stage Two: Seclusion

Second, the officials would put the young women under the custody of Hegai, the king's eunuch in charge of the harem in Susa. The harem referred to the palace women (including concubines and slaves) as well as the area where they lived. They would be taken from their homes and confined to the harem for the remainder of their lives. They would live in splendor but away from the rest of the world, treated more as things than as persons. Any plans they or their parents had would be forfeited.

Stage Three: Beauty Treatments

Third, the candidates would receive beauty treatments with all kinds of ointments and cosmetics to make them attractive for the king's enjoyment and display. Foreign women would be changed to meet Persian standards. The beauty treatment would take an entire year (2:12).

Stage Four: King's Appraisal

Fourth, the king would appraise the candidates. The young woman who pleased the king would be queen instead of Vashti. This plan appealed to him, so he set it in motion immediately.

Truth: God Providentially Uses World Powers to Accomplish His Purposes

God used Joseph's jealous brothers to bring him to Egypt so God's people would be safe until strong enough to conquer Canaan (Genesis 37–50). God prepared Moses for the Exodus through education in the ways of Egypt (Exodus 2; Acts 7:22). God named Cyrus, a pagan, as his servant more than 150 years before he rose to power (Isaiah 44:21–45:13).

Who but the one true God is able to foretell the future

and has the power to accomplish what he has foretold? Isaiah repeatedly affirmed (ten times in chapters 45–46) that there is no God beside the Lord:

> Remember this . . . I am God, and there is no other;
>   I am God, and there is none like me,
> declaring the end from the beginning
>   and from ancient times things not yet done,
> saying, "My counsel shall stand,
>   and I will accomplish all my purpose,"
>
> . . . .
>
> I have spoken, and I will bring it to pass;
>   I have purposed, and I will do it. (46:8–11)

In the midst of every situation, God remains faithful and true to his character and purposes for his people. He is present and working for his glory and their good, enabling his people to stand firm while also showing respect to the ungodly around them.

If you are a Christian, what is God's purpose for you? (See Romans 8:28–30; 1 Peter 1:15–16; 2:13–17.) How might God be using the world's powers and ways to accomplish it? If you are not a Christian, perhaps God has brought you to this place to investigate the claims of Christ. Will you?

Esther's Entrance into the Harem (2:5–14)

Esther's Family (2:5–7)

Esther, an orphan, was among the Jewish exiles in Susa. She was born in Persia, and her family consisted of her cousin, Mordecai, who raised her as his adopted daughter.

Mordecai's ancestors were exiled during the reign of Jeconiah, the second-to-last king of Judah, who was deported to Babylon in 597 BC, 114 years before these events.[1] Through Jair, Mordecai was related to Kish, the father of King Saul (1 Samuel 9:1–2), who had refused to kill King Agag of the Amalekites and incurred the Lord's disfavor. Agag's descendants became enemies of the Jews (we will meet his descendant Haman in the next chapter). Mordecai was probably a second- or third- generation exile who would have known life only as an exile. Why was he still in Susa after Cyrus issued the edict to return to Jerusalem (Ezra 1)? It seems that God had not stirred him or his ancestors to go up to rebuild it (Ezra 1:5). Nevertheless, he was still a Jew; he lived in the Persian culture without being assimilated into it. Since he lived in the citadel, he was probably a Persian official, which explains his freedom to move about the palace area that we see later in the narrative.[2] He was able to serve the Persian king faithfully without denying his first loyalty to the living God. God had work for him to do in Persia.

The name *Esther* is Persian; her Hebrew name was *Hadassah*. Esther, like Mordecai, had to live in two worlds. They were Jews, God's people, in the Persian Empire. Like God's people everywhere, at some point she would be called to decide what defined her—God and his eternal purposes or the earthly kingdom in which she lived. The decision to be defined as God's person may be costly in this life but will be rewarded in eternity. Jesus said, "For whoever would save his life will lose it, but whoever loses his life for my sake will find it. For what will it profit a man if he gains the whole world and forfeits his soul? Or what shall a man give in return for his soul?" (Matthew 16:25–26).

1. Study note on Esther 2:6 in the *ESV® Study Bible* (Wheaton, IL: Crossway, 2008).
2. Study note on Esther 2:5 in *The Reformation Study Bible* (Orlando, FL: Reformation Trust Publishing, 2015).

Esther's Favor with Hegai (2:8–9)

Esther was taken into the king's palace and put in the custody of Hegai, the harem chief. Did she go willingly? Did she have an option? It is unlikely that she could resist. As with any choice, there would be consequences. To refuse the king had meant Vashti was no longer queen. Some have suggested that Esther could have appealed to the harem chief for special treatment on the basis of her Jewish heritage, as Daniel and his three friends did one hundred years earlier (Daniel 1). That is certainly a possibility. However, she was different from Daniel and his three friends; they were among the first exiled group and still had roots in Jerusalem. Esther had never known her homeland, and thus Persian customs were not so strange and unsettling for her. Furthermore, she may have had less opportunity as a young woman than those young men.

In any case, Esther submitted to being chosen a candidate for queen, and her demeanor pleased Hegai. However, the story of Esther is a narrative that tells how God used two of his exiled people to save the Jews at a point in history. It is not primarily a book that teaches how God's people are to live. We must be careful not to draw core beliefs from historical narrative. There are differences in what the Bible records and what it teaches. If Esther had revealed her heritage or refused to be part of the contest for queen, God's purposes for his people would still have been accomplished. However, the story might have been different.

What was it about Esther that pleased Hegai? She "had a beautiful figure and was lovely to look at," but so were all of the candidates (Esther 2:7). Perhaps he found her more attractive because of her demeanor. Unlike Vashti, she was compliant and submissive. It seems that she worked to win the contest. She grew in wisdom and knowledge of her situation and did what pleased those in charge of her beauty treatment. In God's providence, Hegai must have discerned that she would please the king, for he gave her special attention toward that end: cosmetics, special portions of food, and seven chosen young maids. He also advanced her and her maids to the best position in the harem in anticipation of her becoming queen.

Esther's Submission to Mordecai (2:10–11)

Mordecai commanded Esther not to reveal her Hebrew nationality. She did not lie about being a Jew; it seems that in the providence of God, no one asked her about it. Later she did tell the king, but the time was not yet right. She likely would have had little opportunity to become queen if she was known to be a Jew. The prejudice against the Jews, a minority people in exile, would make her and her people a target. Mordecai must have been concerned for her safety as he daily checked on her. She was truly submissive to Mordecai, obeying him even when she was not with him. She carried that trait into the harem. She apparently knew when to speak and when to remain silent. Does that describe you? Sometimes God wants us to be silent when he intends to speak or for a season until he acts.

Esther's Special Preparation for Meeting the King (2:12–14)

Esther received special preparation for her first audience with the king. For one year, she had special beauty treatment at the spa of all spas. Six months with oil of myrrh protected her skin from the sun, keeping it smooth and silky soft. Six months with spices and ointments would counter body odors and provide hygienic cleansing. Special food would bring her to the desired standard for the king's pleasure.

Her special treatment would mean nothing if she did not learn how to approach the king. She would have only one opportunity to win his attention and affection. She would have one evening visit and then return, possibly forever, to a different part of the harem reserved for concubines. After that one visit, if she were not chosen as queen or at least a favored concubine, her only male contact would be Shaashgaz, the king's eunuch in charge of the concubines. "After the king had taken them once to his bed, they were looked on as secondary wives or concubines, were maintained by the king accordingly, and were not allowed to marry."[3] Only the king's specific request would let her visit him again. She would either be queen or the king's property and a perpetual widow.

Truth: God's Redeemed People Live in Two Worlds but Are Defined by One of Them

God's redeemed people live in a world opposed to God and his ways. Even though they live in the world, Jesus said that they are not of the world (John 15:18–19). Paul explained, "Do not be conformed to this world, but be transformed by the renewal of your mind, that by testing you may discern what is the will of God, what is good and acceptable and perfect" (Romans 12:2). God's people are to be defined by their union with Christ (Colossians 3:1–17). This means likeness to his character and power by his Spirit (Romans 8:28–30). Christians view their earthly life from the perspective of being seated with God in the heavenly places in Christ Jesus (Ephesians 2:6). In order to glorify God, at some point they will have to determine to be identified as God's people and defined by God's truth.

---

3. Martin H. Manser, ed., *The New Matthew Henry Commentary* (Grand Rapids: Zondervan, 2010), 589.

What is your mindset? We may feel preferred over others because of our wealth or position, which is pride. We may idolize the things we possess or our reputation. Our possessions may lead us to depend on ourselves, not realizing our need for God. The seduction of wealth causes us to lose our focus on God's call and his preeminence. On the other hand, worldly advantage may be God's way of enabling you to further His kingdom by your generosity and hospitality. What have you learned about being in Christ from the Scriptures in this lesson? If you are in Christ, how might God use your life in the world to aid his people and further his purpose of redeeming a people for himself? Not everyone is called to a high worldly position. But all Christians are called to be faithful in the places God has put them, trusting him each moment and living for his glory instead of their own.

Esther's Favor with the King (2:15–18)

In preparation for her night with the king, each virgin could choose something to take on her visit to the king. Esther heeded the advice of Hegai about what to take with her; he would have insight into what would please the king. "Esther was winning favor in the eyes of all who saw her" (2:15b), but God gave her the desire to listen and learn from them. Four years after the removal of Vashti, in the tenth month of the seventh year of the king's reign, Esther was taken to the king in his royal palace. The king loved Esther more than all the women. She won grace and favor in his sight more than all the other virgins in the contest. The contest was over. The king had found his new queen.

King Ahasuerus set the royal crown on her head and made her queen. In her honor, the king held a great feast for all the officials and servants. Esther's feast was likely comparable to the seven-day feast in chapter 1. The entire empire benefited from the generosity of the king. The *ESV Study Bible* says, "Remission of taxes was a customary form of celebration referred to by Herodotus in his history of the Persian Empire. The generous gifts were probably in the form of food to the poor so that all could share in the celebrations."[4]

Mordecai's Heroism (2:19–23)

Once again, we see the providence of God as we find Mordecai sitting at the king's gate. Probably he held an official position in the service of the king due to Esther's influence in the palace.[5] Esther continued to obey Mordecai by not making known her Jewish roots. Two of the king's eunuchs, Bigthan and Teresh, responsible to guard the king's threshold (the entrance to his private quarters), were angry with the king. Mordecai just "happened to be" in the right place at the right time to hear of their plan to lay hands on the king. He reported the plot to Esther, who told the king in the name of Mordecai. The loyalty of both Esther and Mordecai confirmed Esther as queen and commended Mordecai to the king as a trustworthy servant.

Upon investigation, the men were found guilty and hanged on the gallows, a common practice. Mordecai's loyalty to the king was "recorded in the book of the chronicles in the presence of the king" (2:23). The *NIV Archaeological Study Bible* says, "Acts of loyalty were ordinarily rewarded immediately and generously by Persian kings, but Mordecai's reward was initially overlooked,

4. Study note on Esther 2:18 in the *ESV® Study Bible*.
5. Ibid., study note on Esther 2:21.

even though his action had been noted."[6] The time to reward Mordecai was not yet right. In the providence of God, it would come later. Long before the moment of deliverance, God providentially prepared the scene and the deliverer of his people.

Truth: Preparing for God's Service May Take Years

God's providential timing was evident in the lives of many biblical characters. Moses lived in Egypt for forty years and in the desert for another forty years before leading the Exodus (Acts 7:23, 30). Joseph was in Egypt for thirteen years before he was ready to interpret Pharaoh's dream and lead the famine relief (Genesis 37:2; 41:46). Perhaps his years in prison protected him from becoming self-confident by teaching him dependence upon his God. David ran from Saul for thirteen years after being anointed as king. Paul spent at least seventeen years in "training" after his Damascus Road conversion as preparation to be the apostle to the Gentiles (Galatians 1:18; 2:1).

In a similar way, God's preparing us for service may include secular education, cultural wisdom, and character development. While Mordecai was not immediately rewarded, he received a greater honor at the time God prescribed for him. God is sovereign and providentially prepares his people to accomplish his purposes for them. He is at work even before the moment of their rise to a position of influence. Such a position may involve an individual, but it may also involve an entire nation or even the whole world.

God's providence is not luck, fate, or coincidence. Those words do not give him glory. He providentially set the scene to preserve his people in the future. God often chooses unlikely

---

6. Study note on Esther 2:21–23 in the *NIV Archaeological Study Bible* (Grand Rapids: Zondervan, 2005).

people to accomplish his purposes. Who would have thought Esther—an orphaned, exiled Jewish woman in the Persian Empire dominated by men—was born to be queen of Persia and deliverer of her people, the Jews? With God, opportunities are not limited by gender, nationality, or economic status. God may even use us in significant ways in spite of our past unfaithfulness to him. God's ways are not like the ways of the world, and he accomplishes his purposes while confounding the world's expectations. Though invisible, God is always at work to prepare his people and circumstances to accomplish his purposes. God does not need us, but he graciously uses us for his glory.

What a gracious God! He allowed my husband, Jim, and me to help start a church in our area. The process seemed long, but God was working in us and others as well as establishing a new church.

God's providence was evident in the planting of the church to which my husband and I belong. God is not limited to one place. He is present in all his fullness in every place at every moment. What he purposes, he also works out. While we were just beginning the process of planting a church in Boerne, Texas, God was working in the heart of a young pastor and his wife in Kearney, Nebraska. They were hearing God's call to become church planters and began investigating the process. It would be five years before our paths crossed. But God was implementing his plan even though we could not see the details. At the perfect time, we would be ready to move forward together.

During those years of waiting, God showed us truths about his person, power, and purposes that would propel us into situations to prove his love and faithfulness. We were on a ride that would make most roller coasters seem tame. God was making us into a community through hard work and fellowship, and he was building our faith through disappointments and times of waiting. Such growth was necessary before we were ready for the responsibilities we would face in a church.

Our pastor-to-be and his family arrived April 28, 2005, for an interview and meetings with our group. By July, he was our called church planter, and we became Trinity Presbyterian Church Plant. By September, God had provided sufficient funds to cover church expenses for the next three years. Our pastor's family bought a home in Boerne the day after selling their home in Nebraska. We celebrated Thanksgiving together two days after they moved into their home. What a great celebration, remembering how God had brought us to that important moment in the life of our church.

We learned much about God's providence as we worked to plant this church. What God pronounces is certain to happen, but it requires faith to believe that he is in the process of accomplishing his will and that it will be good. Nothing is impossible with God. God is not pressured by our fears or circumstances but works in his time and way. God simultaneously works on different fronts, some visible and others invisible. As I write this book ten years later, our church has helped plant another church in a neighboring town and has moved into its own permanent facility. We are certain that whatever comes, God will reveal that he has already been there and has prepared us for it. We rest in our God and his providence.

How have you seen God's providence in your life to save you and prepare you to serve him? Recall past failures and previous blessings that prepared you to serve him today. Your present circumstances are God's means for your sanctification. What can you do to become more discerning about God's providence in your life? Consider the words of "God Moves in a Mysterious Way." What mysterious ways in your life come to mind? Write them down now and ask God how he has prepared you to know, love, and serve him through these very mysterious ways. Will you step out in faith to do so?

Closing Prayer

Lord God, your purposes ripen fast when my eyes are opened to see them. Each moment I see your hand in my life and in the lives of other individuals and nations. Sometimes the answer to my prayers is bitter to my taste. Give me faith to believe that sweet will be the flower that is the fruit of those answers. I trust you to interpret such works according to your perfection and to make them plain in your time. For your glorious name. Amen.

Haman's Rise to Power

And when Haman saw that Mordecai did not bow down
or pay homage to him, Haman was filled with fury. . . .
So . . . Haman sought to destroy all the Jews, the people
of Mordecai, throughout the whole kingdom of Ahasuerus. (Esther 3:5–6)

Text

Esther 3

Truth

God's providential love for his people is greater than evil
plots against them.

Hymn: "Though Troubles Assail Us"

Though troubles assail us and dangers affright,
Though friends should all fail us and foes all unite,

Yet one thing secures us, whatever betide,
The promise assures us, "The Lord will provide."

The birds, without garner or storehouse, are fed;
From them let us learn to trust God for our bread.
His saints what is fitting shall ne'er be denied
So long as 'tis written, "The Lord will provide."

When Satan assails us to stop up our path,
And courage all fails us, we triumph by faith.
He cannot take from us, though oft he has tried,
This heart-cheering promise, "The Lord will provide."

No strength of our own and no goodness we claim;
Yet, since we have known of the Savior's great name,
In this our strong tower for safety we hide:
The Lord is our power, "The Lord will provide."

—JOHN NEWTON, 1779

Opening Prayer

Lord God, thank you for your providential love and mighty power that overthrows evil plots against your people and your plan for them. I have no strength of my own; I rest on you, my great God and Father. Please continue to open my eyes to see your providence in history and in my own life. May your revelation give me hope and joy. For your glory, Amen.

Questions for Study and Discussion

Growing Conflict

▶ READ ESTHER 3:1–6

1. To what does "After these things" (2:1; 3:1) refer? See 2:16; 3:7.

2. Using the following Scriptures, list some facts about Haman's family background.

   a. Exodus 17:8–16

   b. Numbers 24:7

c. Deuteronomy 25:17–19

d. 1 Samuel 15

3. How did the king honor Haman?

4. What did Mordecai do to incur the anger of Haman?

5. Why do you think Mordecai acted in this way, considering the effect it would have on Haman?

6. What does Haman's expression of rage reveal about his character and attitude toward Mordecai?

A Good Plan Thwarted

▶ READ ESTHER 3:7–15

7. How long did it take Haman to approach the king (v. 7), and what effect might this time delay have had on Haman?

8. What do you learn about Haman from his approach to the king (vv. 8–10) and his plan?

9. What are the main points in Haman's plan?

10. What thoughts do you have about the king and his response to Haman's request?

The Scheming of Man and the Providence of God

▶ REVIEW ESTHER 3

11. What do you learn about the characters of King Ahasuerus and Haman in this chapter?

12. How does the gospel of God's grace in Christ help you overcome temptations to be like one of them?

13. What are God's purposes for Christians?

14. What lessons about God's plan and your own life have you learned from this chapter?

15. What evil schemes against you and your growth as a Christian are you experiencing today? How might God use them to make you more like the Lord Jesus Christ?

16. How does this chapter encourage you to trust God's providence in your life?

17. Write a prayer of gratitude to God for his providential care in your life based on your answers to the above questions.

Commentary

Have you ever felt that for every step you take forward, you follow with two backward? You finally make an inroad with a relationship, your work, or your church, and without warning you hit a wall or encounter resistance. In the great story of Esther, we have seen the sovereign hand of God in her selection as queen and the record of Mordecai's loyalty. But just when it seems everything is working according to plan, enter Haman, the high-ranking political advisor or prime minister to the king. He is the villain or main antagonist to Esther's influence in the kingdom, and he is determined to wield his power to his own advantage. Esther used her influence on behalf of her people, the Jews; Haman used his to plan their mass murder.

What a picture of life! When God's people move forward, they immediately come under attack. But God is sovereign, and his purposes are always accomplished. It is foolish to fight against God and his people. He has no equal. In fact, he even uses attempts to thwart his purposes as the means to accomplish them. God's love for his people is greater than evil plots against them.

The Setting (3:1)

"After these things. . . ." To what things do the opening words of chapter 3 refer? Esther has been queen for five years (2:16; 3:7). Mordecai has foiled the plans of Bigthan and Teresh to kill the king (2:19–23). Now King Ahasuerus made a big decision. He advanced Haman above all the officials in the kingdom.

Haman's Appointment (3:2–6)

Who is Haman? He is called "the Agagite." Agag was king of the Amalekites, ancient enemies of the Jews before they entered Canaan (Exodus 17:8–16) and after settling there (Numbers 24:7; Deuteronomy 25:17–19). He was defeated by King Saul and killed by Samuel (1 Samuel 15). It is possible that Haman and Mordecai inherited this long-standing feud.

Haman is also called the son of Hammedatha, who is mentioned only in the book of Esther. The name *Hammedatha* is of Persian etymology, signifying "given by the moon."[1] Perhaps Haman thought himself a god! Certainly his promotion and advancement above his peers fed his arrogance. The king must

1. James Orr, ed., "Hammedatha," *The International Standard Bible Encyclopedia* (Chicago: The Howard-Severance Company, 1915). This public domain resource can be found at www.biblestudytools.com.

have been assured of his loyalty and perhaps had discerned some leadership qualities in him. His high office seems to be the same one later given to Mordecai.

The king commanded his servants to bow down and pay Haman homage. Bowing to a superior was normal court etiquette in Persian culture; it was not necessarily an act of worship.[2] However, Mordecai refused to bow down to Haman. Although Mordecai had instructed Esther not to reveal their Jewish heritage, now he used it as a reason for not giving honor to this high official. Day after day the king's officials asked him, "Why do you transgress the king's command?" (3:3). Yet he repeatedly refused to listen to them. Why? If Haman was claiming divine honor, bowing to him would be idolatry. Culturally, Abraham bowed to the Hittites (Genesis 23:7), and when Isaac blessed Jacob he said that his mother's sons would bow down to him (Genesis 27:29). This was different; no self-respecting Jew would bow before an enemy of his people—no, rather, we should say that no God-fearing Jew would bow before an enemy of his God! In revealing his Jewish heritage, Mordecai broke his own command to Esther. It seems that the Persians did not yet know he was a Jew or related to Esther.

Finally, the king's officials reported Mordecai to Haman to see if his Jewish "excuse" would stand. Haman the Agagite raged at their report. That Mordecai was a Jew ignited Haman's rage. "But he disdained to lay hands on Mordecai alone" (3:6). Mordecai alone was not even worthy of his consideration. Haman's fury spread to all the Jews. His injured pride could not be balanced by punishing one man. He wanted to exterminate all of

2. Study note on Esther 3:2–4 in the *ESV® Study Bible* (Wheaton, IL: Crossway, 2008).

them. Little did Haman realize that he was playing right into God's purposes for delivering the Jews.

Haman's response was a manifestation of spiritual warfare that began in Eden (Genesis 3)—warfare against God's people and God's eternal plan for his kingdom on earth. The Assyrians (701 BC) taunted the people of Jerusalem to doubt God's trustworthiness and abandon their faith in him (Isaiah 36–37). At the time of Christ's birth, Herod the Great ordered the killing of all Hebrew boys two years old and under because this "king of the Jews" posed a threat to his throne. There was a bigger threat that Herod may not have realized. The chief priests and scribes had reported to Herod that this child was the promised Christ who was to be born in Bethlehem (Micah 5:2; Matthew 2:5). If Jesus were killed, God's redemptive plan through him would have been thwarted (Matthew 2:1–18). During World War II, Adolph Hitler, like Haman, targeted the Jewish race for extermination. At the present, Christians are being killed for refusing to recant their belief in Jesus Christ. If you are a Christian, expect spiritual warfare aimed at destroying your Christian faith and witness, and perhaps even you. Nevertheless, God has not left you alone. Be prepared to stand in the armor God has given you (Ephesians 6:10–20), confident that his purposes cannot be thwarted. In fact, Satan's attempts to stop God's plan for you and his kingdom may become the very means by which it is accomplished.

Truth: God Displays His Sovereign Power through Evil Assaults against His People

Early in the history of mankind, Eve succumbed to the temptation by the serpent (Genesis 3). God responded with the announcement of the evil tempter's defeat by a future redeemer who would be an offspring of Eve (3:15).

Generations later, Joseph's jealous brothers sold him into slavery (Genesis 37–50). Though loyal to his master, he was imprisoned because of refusing his master's wife, who falsely accused him. For seventeen years he never saw his family. Yet at the end of his life he said to his brothers, "As for you, you meant evil against me, but God meant it for good, to bring it about that many people should be kept alive, as they are today" (Genesis 50:20).

Matthew 4:1–11 records how Satan tempted Jesus to use his divine powers to prove he was the Son of God. He also tempted Jesus to claim God's kingdom immediately by worshiping him, a violation of the first commandment given to Moses in Exodus 20. His method was the same as in Genesis 3. He twisted God's words to his advantage, but he did not succeed with Jesus. Satan must have known the prophecy in Isaiah 52:13–53:12, which included the human suffering and death of Jesus on the cross. If Jesus had succumbed to any of these temptations, he would have failed to accomplish God's plan for his perfect human life and sacrificial death on the cross. Throughout his ministry, people tried to trap Jesus into displaying his deity apart from his human suffering and death. The officials, passersby, and criminals at his crucifixion taunted him to come down from the cross to prove he was the Son of God (Luke 23:32–43). Jesus knew these satanic assaults against him were part of God's eternal plan of redemption. He refused to give in to them.

Christians should expect assaults aimed at their relationship with God. We are set apart for God and set apart from sin and the world through union with Jesus Christ our Lord. He is the sovereign authority of our lives; we are not to substitute an earthly authority figure for him. In what ways are you experiencing an assault against your union with Jesus Christ? How is God working for your good through these assaults? God is sovereign over every detail of your life. His power is at work on your behalf as you remain true to him and his purposes for you in the face of persecution.

Listen to what Ashley writes about God's using evil to bring her to a life of trust in him:

By God's great providence, I grew up in a Christian home. At age eleven, I received Christ as my Savior, but as a teen I rebelled against God. In my early twenties, against God's will and my family's counsel, I dated and fell in love with an alcoholic nonbeliever. Blind to his alcoholism, we quickly married and started a family. Upon realizing I was expecting, I wanted God's best for my son and me. I recognized my glaring rebellion against God. Yet in his grace he accepted my confession of sin and forgave me. I recommitted my life to him.

However, my husband's alcoholism increasingly damaged our lives. He suffered several job losses. We sank into poverty. My son and I began living in fear. Through several unsettling events, God showed me that my only protective recourse was divorce. When I was penniless, homeless, and unemployed, God providentially began unfolding his gracious plans for us. God provided a home, a job, and a Christian preschool. When I was fearful of my ex-husband's raging alcoholic influence on my son, God comforted me through Scripture and prayer. God has protected my son. He hasn't seen his father in over a year, yet God has provided several godly father figures—uncles and a grandfather that frequently build into his life. God led us to a wonderful Bible-centered church where our relationships with God are nurtured. He has transformed my fearful son into a joyous child of faith in Jesus Christ. My son and I now live a peaceful, God-filled life. We strive to live God's will. We are blessed!

Haman's Plot (3:7–11)

Haman was furious! He had to get rid of Mordecai and the Jews, but he could not destroy this entire group of people without the king's permission. Haman took an entire year to cast lots (the Pur) daily to determine the best time to approach the king (3:7). Casting lots to determine the day for implementing his plan was a normal way to seek guidance in his culture. Though festering within, Haman begrudgingly waited for the right moment. With each day his rage grew and his bitterness deepened. A plan of such magnitude would need time and careful planning. Finally, after twelve months, Haman decided it was time to speak to the king.

Haman was the power behind the throne, a master of hidden agenda and power plays. He approached the king on the basis of concern for the king's welfare. "There is a certain people scattered abroad and dispersed among the peoples in all the provinces of your kingdom. Their laws are different from those of every other people, and they do not keep the king's laws, so that it is not to the king's profit to tolerate them" (3:8). What law had they not kept? Haman's greatest concern was that Mordecai had not bowed to him. Haman's half-truth condemned all the Jews. He suggested that the king issue a decree that this "certain people" be destroyed. Haman never mentioned that the people were the Jews, and the king did not ask.

Haman appealed next to the king's greed. If the king's tolerating them was unprofitable to the king, how would obliterating them profit him? "The remission of taxes [in conjunction with Esther's crowning, 2:18] and the unsuccessful war with Greece may have left the royal treasury low on funds."[3] Haman offered to pay 10,000 talents of silver to put into the king's treasuries. This was an enormous amount of silver: 12 million ounces,[4] "almost two-thirds of the annual income of the empire. Presumably the money would have come from the plundered wealth of the victims of the decree."[5]

The king liked the idea. He immediately gave Haman his signet ring and permission to destroy the Jews and to use as much of the silver as he needed. Giving Haman his signet ring was tantamount to giving him the highest authority in the land, which was necessary to issue a decree to accomplish his wicked plot.

Remember, the king did not know his wife, Esther, was a Jew and would come under this edict. Neither did Haman know this. But Haman had not mentioned the Jews by name, only "a certain people." Ahasuerus delegated his supreme power to the evil Haman without asking any questions about the people and without knowing the full consequences of his decision.

Truth: God Accomplishes His Purposes through the Evil Schemes of Powerful People

Power itself is not necessarily evil; abuse of power at the expense of others is. Pride and self-exaltation are at the root of corrupt use of power. In ourselves, we have no hope against such evil. But our God is the only omnipotent, omniscient being. No one and nothing can stop his purposes. Though evil surrounds us, God actually accomplishes his purposes through the evil schemes of powerful people.

3. Ibid., study note on Esther 3:8.
4. Ibid., study note on Esther 3:9.
5. Study note on Esther 3:9 in the *NIV Archaeological Study Bible* (Grand Rapids: Zondervan, 2005).

What are God's purposes for Christians? He commands us to be holy and works all things for our good—to make us like his own Son. If we are to share in the glory of Christ, then we must first share in his suffering. However, God promises to be with us. We need not fear that God will forsake us, for Jesus was forsaken by God in our place when he bore our sins in his body on the cross (Matthew 27:46; 1 Peter 2:24). Nothing and no one can separate us from the love of God that is ours in Christ Jesus (Romans 8:31–39). What evil schemes against you and your growth as a Christian are you experiencing today? How might God use them to make you more like the Lord Jesus Christ?

Haman's Edict (3:12–15)

At last Haman was ready to implement his plan. One month after receiving permission, Haman summoned the scribes on the thirteenth day of the first month (Nisan). This was the day before the Passover (Exodus 12:1–6). How ironic that while the Jews were preparing to celebrate God's deliverance of them from Egypt, Haman was preparing to destroy them. Who would win?

The scribes wrote an edict according to Haman's orders. Notice the use of "all" and "every." Haman left no stone unturned. According to Frank Gaebelein the edict was written to the king's "satraps, who ruled over twenty major divisions of the empire; the governors, who ruled smaller subdivisions of satrapies; and the nobles [officials], who served under the governors and were perhaps chiefs of the conquered peoples."[6] Every province received the edict in its own script and every people in their own language.

6. Frank E. Gaebelein, ed., *1 & 2 Kings, 1 & 2 Chronicles, Ezra, Nehemiah, Esther, Job,* The Expositor's Bible Commentary, vol. 4 (Grand Rapids: Zondervan, 1988), 814.

Being written in the name of the king and sealed with the king's signet ring meant that the edict had the king's authority. The comprehensive instructions were to destroy, kill, and annihilate all Jews—young, old, men, women, and children—in one day and to plunder their goods. (This may have been the source of the 10,000 talents pledged by Haman.) At the king's order, couriers went out hurriedly, proclaiming to all the people in every province the decree that they should be ready for that day, the thirteenth day of the twelfth month. The decree was also issued in Susa, the citadel.

What a travesty of justice! Haman's intense hatred and bitterness rang through the all-inclusive decree: all provinces, all peoples, every script, every language—kill all, plunder all. Haman was not the only despicable character in this narrative. Did King Ahasuerus bother to evaluate the accusations? Did he care about an entire people group being annihilated? Why did he reward Haman instead of Mordecai, who had saved his life? How could he let the financial benefit—a huge payoff to allow the genocide of the Jews—influence his decision?

The characters of these two men were quite evident as they sat down to drink while "the city of Susa was thrown into confusion" (Esther 3:15). Why the confusion? *The Reformation Study Bible* explains, "The city, not just the administrative classes in the citadel, is in a highly agitated state. There is probably a measure of sympathy for the Jews, but equally there is surely bewilderment as to what the future might hold for other people groups as a result of Haman's influence over the emperor."[7] The edict was irreversible. It seemed nothing could be done.

7. Study note on Esther 3:15 in *The Reformation Study Bible* (Orlando, FL: Reformation Trust Publishing 2015), 743.

But the Jews were God's people. "The lot is cast into the lap, but its every decision is from the LORD" (Proverbs 16:33). In the face of impossible circumstances and evil people, it is good to remember, "But God!" Haman made his plan, but the Lord established his steps (Proverbs 16:9). Haman could go only as far as God allowed him to go. God was in control.

Truth: God Will Not Allow His People to Be Eradicated by His Enemies

God is greater than evil perpetrated against his people. The contrast between good and evil is stark in this chapter. In the midst of this evil scheme, the exiles would experience God's protection, provision, and purpose to maintain their special identity as his people. Annually they would recount their history of this event (Esther 9:20–32). Even though Christians die at the hands of terrorists and natural disasters, they are secure in God's saving power in Christ Jesus. Death, our worst enemy, has already been conquered on the cross by Jesus. Where are you faced with the temptation to fear and doubt God's loving care? How does the truth of God's love and providence encourage you? Take time right now to worship him as your sovereign God, your protector, and your provider.

Closing Prayer

Gracious God, how precious it is to know that you are sovereign and that you protect your people. In the midst of confusion, you provide insight. When facing danger, you are my shield and protector. No evil words or plots to destroy your people can separate me from your love that has been demonstrated in Christ Jesus, my Lord. I do not understand the forces of evil in our world or the suffering your people endure. I acknowledge that many around the world are killed because of their witness to your Son, Jesus Christ. But I trust the truth that you are God and there is no other. You know the future, and you use the evil attempts of evil people to accomplish your purposes for your glory and my good. May I stand firmly on what I know and not be distracted or discouraged by what is unclear. In the name of Jesus Christ, my Lord and Savior. Amen.

The Moment for Esther

I will go to the king, though it is against the law, and if
I perish, I perish. (Esther 4:16)

Text

Esther 4

Truth

God providentially uses confusion and chaos to develop
faith in his people.

Hymn: "I Know Whom I Have Believed"

I know not why God's wondrous grace
To me he has made known,
Nor why, unworthy, Christ in love
Redeemed me for his own.

Refrain:
But "I know whom I have believed,
And am persuaded that he is able
To keep that which I've committed
Unto him against that day."

I know not how this saving faith
To me he did impart,
Nor how believing in his Word
Wrought peace within my heart. *Refrain*

I know not how the Spirit moves,
Convincing men of sin,
Revealing Jesus through the Word,
Creating faith in him. *Refrain*

I know not what of good or ill
May be reserved for me,
Of weary ways or golden days,
Before his face I see. *Refrain*

I know not when my Lord may come,
At night or noonday fair,
Nor if I'll walk the vale with him,
Or "meet him in the air." *Refrain*

—DANIEL W. WHITTLE, 1883

Opening Prayer

All-wise, sovereign God, I acknowledge my weakness and fear in the face of confusion, chaos, and despair. To whom can I turn but you? I turn to you this day to know your character and your will that I may live through faith in you. You are Providence; nothing happening today has escaped your notice. In fact, you are sovereign, and you orchestrate what is best for me and for your glory. Teach me more of what that means as I look at the defining moment for Esther. In the mighty name of Jesus. Amen.

Questions for Study and Discussion

An Edict and Disaster

▶ READ ESTHER 4:1–14

1. How did Mordecai and the Jews react to the king's edict?

2. What do you learn about their kind of reaction from the following verses: Nehemiah 9:1; Isaiah 15:3; Jeremiah 6:26; 49:3; Ezekiel 27:31; Jonah 3:5–6; Matthew 11:21?

3. Why do you think Esther was distressed by the reports from her attendants?

4. Describe Hathach's mission. Was it successful? Explain your answer from these verses.

5. Try to picture Hathach running back and forth between Esther and Mordecai. Explain the conversation between Esther and Mordecai.

6. God's overarching purpose for his people is that they glorify and enjoy him forever. What enemies of God are scheming to thwart this purpose for you?

7. What will you do to relate to God daily to know, glorify, and enjoy him?

A Plan to Respond to the Edict

▶ READ ESTHER 4:15–17

8. What did Esther need before she would obey Mordecai's command?

9. What did Esther ask Mordecai to do for her? Why?

10. How does her request show that she had not lost all of her Jewish roots? (See 1 Samuel 1:7–10; 2 Samuel 12:16–17; Ezra 8:23; Isaiah 58:2–5; Daniel 9:3.)

11. How does Esther's response show both courage and submission?

12. Describe the relationship between Mordecai and Esther.

13. What lessons do you learn from Esther and Mordecai about being an active part of God's saving his people?

14. Where do you need wisdom and courage to serve God on behalf of his people?

15. How are people able to approach God without fear? Use John 14:6; Hebrews 4:16; 10:19–23; and any other applicable Scriptures.

16. How is God using your present circumstances to develop your faith in him?

17. Write a prayer asking God to direct you. The words of "I Know Whom I Have Believed" might help you.

Commentary

Confusion, chaos, and despair describe the emotions of people around the world after a tsunami, earthquake, terrorist attack, or execution of Christians by ISIS terrorists. The same words described the people of Susa as they heard Haman's abominable edict issued in the name of the king. What were they to do? Who would rise up to help them? Would God's people turn to God as they were stirred by the news? In the midst of such crises, God sovereignly works on behalf of his people. He uses confusion and chaos to develop their faith. He tests faith and commitment by asking them to do the impossible.

Reactions to the King's Edict (4:1–5)

Mourning: Mordecai and the Jews (4:1–3)

Mordecai, upon hearing what had been done, "tore his clothes and put on sackcloth and ashes, and went out into the midst of the city, and he cried out with a loud and bitter cry" (4:1). According to Merrill Tenney, this was the traditional way of expressing grief in Jewish culture. Sackcloth was a strong, rough cloth from the long, dark hair of an Oriental goat or camel. It was the proper garb for serious or sober occasions. Its dark color was fitting for times of grief and sadness. It was also the mark of abject penitence. The roughness of the garment was an aid to self-chastisement; tossing ashes over it accentuated the mourner's distress.[1] Mordecai went to the entrance of the king's gate but was allowed to go no further. It is reasonable that such an appearance would be unacceptable in the palace in light of the pomp described in earlier chapters.

Wherever the king's decree was read in every province, the Jews also mourned greatly with fasting, weeping, and lamenting. Like Mordecai, they donned sackcloth and ashes. Such mourning was an indicator of penitence called for by God in Jeremiah 6:26 and demonstrated by penitent Jews in the reformation under Nehemiah (9:1). Jesus also spoke of wearing sackcloth and ashes (Matthew 11:21). However, this chapter has no mention of the prayer that normally accompanied such mourning among the Jews. Nothing to this point indicates that Esther and Mordecai were devout people of faith in God, so it is not clear whether they prayed to him. Nevertheless, in times

---

1. Merrill C. Tenney, ed., "Sackcloth," in *The Zondervan Pictorial Encyclopedia of the Bible*, vol. 5 (Grand Rapids: Zondervan, 1976).

of calamity people who do not regularly pray sometimes cry out for protection and deliverance. God's purpose for them would be accomplished whether they prayed or not.

Investigation: Esther (4:4–5)

Esther was deeply distressed by the report from the young women and eunuchs attending her. She sought to determine why Mordecai mourned. She sent garments to clothe Mordecai, but he refused to accept them. Most certainly, she feared for his safety, but she also realized he could not enter the palace wearing sackcloth and ashes. Even if he could, he would not be allowed in Esther's quarters.

Why did Esther not know what was happening? Was bad news not allowed in the king's palace? Since she was not known as a Jew, did they assume she would not care about this group of people? Though Esther was the queen, she did not have direct access to the king or to the news of the kingdom. She was confined to the palace, isolated from the world outside. She had to rely on an intermediary. Desiring to communicate with Mordecai, she sent Hathach to learn from Mordecai what was happening and why.

Hathach must have proven to be trustworthy or Esther would not have sent him on this important mission. It is likely that he had learned of Esther's Jewish nationality through being the messenger between her and Mordecai. Can you picture Hathach running back and forth between them? With each step, their hearts must have raced faster as they faced the possibility that Hathach was more faithful to the king than to Esther. Fear and doubt are powerful emotions when left unchecked. So also is a mind left to wander into vain imaginations. As they each waited in turn for Hathach to come back with an answer, did their thoughts turn to what would happen to them if the king found out about Esther's heritage? They were in a situation ripe with opportunities to think of everything except God. Without an anchor for their thoughts, their emotions would run wild.

Truth: God's People Have Access to God in Every Circumstance

God's enemies are always scheming to thwart God's plan for his people. In the midst of adversity, God is always available to his people. Confidence to approach God is developed before the test comes, however. God's plan or purpose for his people is for them to glorify and enjoy him forever. This means to look to him personally moment by moment. A. W. Tozer wrote, "*God wills that we should push on into His Presence and live our whole life there.* This is to be known to us in conscious experience. It is more than a doctrine to be held, it is a life to be enjoyed every moment of every day."[2] What is keeping you from enjoying God's presence and relating to him personally?

How does one relate personally to God? The only way is through faith alone in Christ alone (John 14:6; 20:31). There are not many ways to God. One does not enter God's presence through belonging to a group or a Christian family. Jesus said that the way to enter the kingdom is narrow and few find it (Matthew 7:13–14). Through him and his sacrificial death alone, one may approach the holy, sovereign God. On what basis do you approach the one true God?

Spending time with God enables you to learn his character, mind, heart, and will for his people. The means he has provided

2. A. W. Tozer, *The Pursuit of God* (Camp Hill, PA: Christian Publications, 1982), 36, italics original.

are Bible study and prayer, church attendance, worship, and service. This is more than a five-minute thought for the day as you rush out the door. The world and the devil try to keep you away from God. They use interruptions, discouragement, doubt, guilt, fear, and "things" that gobble up your time and energy. Keeping you away from God puts you back in your default mode—self. Self keeps you from recognizing sin, running to God for forgiveness, and being filled with his Spirit. It keeps you from enjoying him as your loving Father and delighting in what pleases him. It keeps you from availing yourself of the access that is yours through faith in Christ. It keeps your focus on anything other than God.

Spending time with God daily helps you to know and enjoy him and prepares you to approach him with confidence in times of great need. In times of crisis, where do you turn first? To God and his Word, to prayer, to worship? To assurance of God's sovereign control, love for his people, and desire for their eternal good? Or to Google, your own strategy, a friend, counselor, doctor . . . ? God has provided other people as resources, and he may direct you to seek help from others as you seek him first.

Mordecai's (and God's) Plan for Esther (4:6–14)

Hathach the Courier (4:6–9)

Hathach met Mordecai in the open square of the city in front of the king's gate. Mordecai explained Haman's intense anger because Mordecai refused to bow before him. He explained the details of the edict, including the exact sum of money Haman would pay into the king's treasuries. He also gave Hathach "a copy of the written decree issued in Susa for their destruction, that he might show it to Esther and explain it to her and command her to go to the king to beg his favor and plead with him on behalf of her people" (4:8). If Hathach had not known that Esther was a Jew, he did now. Mordecai, unable to deliver this important message, entrusted it to another. Hathach was asked to do something difficult; he, the servant, was to command the queen. He faithfully relayed Mordecai's message to Esther.

Mordecai had one aim in mind: impress upon Esther the urgency of the situation. He had all the facts, but he was powerless to intervene as he had with Bigthan and Teresh. He was looking to Esther to intervene with King Ahasuerus, expecting deliverance from the palace. Some suggest that Mordecai had not looked to God for deliverance. Others suggest that his approach to Esther came in answer to prayer. In either case, God was working behind the scenes to deliver his people. His faithfulness was not dependent on theirs.

Growing Tension (4:10–11)

The tension grew as Esther commanded Hathach to explain her dire situation to Mordecai. The king had not summoned her for thirty days. Possibly the king was losing interest in Esther. If so, this would make her situation even more perilous. Yet there was one glimmer of hope. The king might extend the golden scepter to her, granting her entrance into his inner court. Esther was not necessarily refusing to go. However, she wanted Mordecai to have all the facts of her situation.

Defining Moment (4:12–14)

Back at the entrance to the king's gate, Hathach relayed Esther's message. She seemed to have few options. She could deny her Jewishness at least for a time, but this would certainly not please God. She could make it known publicly and be seen as "not to the king's profit" (3:8). She could go to the king and possibly die for entering without being summoned. She could refuse to go and face certain death along with her father's family when Haman's edict was enforced. Being queen would not protect her from the king's irrevocable edict. If the king did not enforce his edict against Esther, he would lose face with his people. It seems unlikely that the king would let anyone, even the queen, bring him disgrace. After all, is that not why he got rid of Vashti? Neither would Haman let Esther stand in his way. He would find a way to get rid of her if he knew she was a Jew. His all-consuming hatred for the Jews would stop at nothing and no one.

I wonder if Esther was thinking, "Are there no other options? None of these sounds good to me." There was no time to waste. Mordecai got right to the point. In effect, he said, "Don't be naive; you will perish with the other Jews if this edict is enforced." Her comfortable place in the palace made no difference. Mordecai seemed to understand God's preservation of his covenant people, the Jews. He planted the idea that Esther could be part of that salvation. It was time for her to be defined as one of God's people.

Truth: The Best Option Always Comes from God

God's plan for his people cannot be thwarted. God providentially works to secure his purposes through all kinds of people. While Mordecai did not mention God to Esther, he believed his people would be delivered by some means if Esther declined to approach the king. His challenge to her was based on God's providence. The present threat—"such a time as this"—may have been the reason for her exaltation as queen (4:14).

God can be trusted to secure his purposes even in the face of extremely dire circumstances. As he does, he often tests and grows our faith and commitment by giving us some seemingly impossible part in bringing about his purposes.

What seemingly impossible task is God asking you to do for him and his people? Is he asking you to take on a responsibility in your church that means giving up something else you want to do? Is he calling you to reach out to others in need, to love an unlovable person, or to forgive one who has hurt you repeatedly? Is he calling you to do the next thing before you with confidence in him and patience to wait for his purpose in it? What will it cost you to do what God has placed before you? What will you miss if you refuse? Perhaps God has put you in this situation "for such a time as this" that you may experience his providential power and care on your behalf. God's call is always the best choice.

Esther's Agreement (4:15–17)

The enormity of the problem facing Esther required wisdom to solve. She needed courage to carry out the solution. She also needed vision to see the importance of the future of her people above her present comfort. God had promised both Abraham (Genesis 12:1–3) and David (2 Samuel 7:12–17) that they would have a descendant to establish a kingdom that would endure forever. God's plan could not be thwarted, but Esther could be an active participant in it only if she agreed to approach the king.

Enlisting the People (4:15–16b)

The problem involved all the Jews in the empire, so Esther asked all Jews to be part of the solution. They were to fast from food and water for three days and nights. Esther and her girls would also fast. While prayer is not mentioned, the intensity of the fasting seems to imply intense prayer with it. Prayer and fasting before God were customary Jewish practices in times of sorrow, anxiety, or penitence (1 Samuel 1:7–10; 2 Samuel 12:16–17; Ezra 8:23; Isaiah 58:2–5; Daniel 9:3).

The reality of the problem was that Esther was asked to go against the law. What happened to those who disobeyed the law? Vashti was removed for defying the king's command (1:19–21). Bigthan and Teresh were hanged (2:21–23). Mordecai showed courage by not bowing to Haman (3:2), resulting in the entire Jewish population in Persia being slated for annihilation (3:13). Would she be next? Esther needed courage. Courage is not a lack of fear but the willingness to take risky, bold steps even when filled with fear and anxiety. She needed mental and moral strength to venture, persevere, withstand, and overcome danger, fear, and difficulty. Courage was necessary to accept the risk of approaching the king on behalf of her people. She would need strength of mind to carry on in spite of the present danger.

Esther's Decision (4:16c–17)

Esther announced her decision: "Then [after three days] I will go to the king, though it is against the law, and if I perish, I perish" (4:16). This was no religious cliché; this was reality. With almost despairing resignation, she demonstrated courage and willing submission. "Mordecai then went away and did everything as Esther had ordered him" (4:17).

Truth: Identification with God and His Purposes Involves Courage and Resolution

God's people today experience crises in our hostile world. They face opposition, personal attack, verbal or physical abuse, prejudice, and terrorism. Like all people, God's people experience unemployment, death, divorce, rape, incest . . . as well as the universal effects of sin: disease, disasters, and so on. But they also face threats from people opposed to God, his purposes, and his people. God may ask his people to leave their place of security to give themselves fully and without reservation to God's people and his plan for them. Living for God's glory and kingdom requires steadfast faith in God and his promises. Failure is not sin, but unbelief is. It is possible to have sound biblical theology yet live without connecting what you profess to believe to the affairs of your life, thus missing the joy of living by faith in your sovereign God.

What kind of crises have you experienced? What do your responses to them reveal about the object of your faith? In whom or what do you trust? Who is your first responder, the first to come to your aid? How might God use your experiences to help his people in distress?

What can you expect from God when he calls you to live by faith, giving your life on behalf of his kingdom and people? God may graciously give powerful, immediate deliverance from a situation. Or he may give grace to persevere in simple trust and obedience when all your hopes are smashed and your dreams evaporate. In either case, living by faith pleases God (Hebrews 11:6). Will you join Esther in saying, "If I perish, I perish"? "I can't" should not be part of your Christian vocabulary when God calls you to help his people.

My friend Peggy has not had immediate deliverance from her sorrow. God has given her faith to persevere and draw courage and comfort from his providence.

Peggy was grieving deeply when she lost her thirty-four-year-old son after a yearlong battle with cancer. She asked me, "Would you mind sharing a few of your favorite psalms or devotional stories with me? I would love to hear the miracles others have felt pass into their lives through the blessing of God's Word. Do you have a friend that has been comforted beyond comfort through God's words in a story you can share? I am reading the Scriptures, and re-reading them, and they are just quiet to me. It's like reading some typeface on a white background, like a grocery list or something. It's like I need somebody to kick-start that part of my heart or my head again. I'm sure that I am a bad Christian or a fake or something. Trust me, I'm really trying, but sometimes I just dry up inside, or maybe my eyes go dry and seeing beyond one inch isn't so possible."

My eyes filled with tears as I cried out to God to direct me over the thin ice of her tender emotions. I needed wisdom to give her God's truth that would encourage her and not add to her sorrow. In her grief, she was asking for help from God, so I pointed her to God and his character in Psalms 23 (Shepherd), 46 (Refuge), and 145 (grace, mercy, love, and many other attributes). By God's grace, twenty years earlier I had clung to his providence in a difficult time, though not the same circumstances as hers. By God's providence, I had written my thoughts and feelings in a journal, and I was able to find it among the many books on my shelf. I sent some thoughts to her, but I was careful not to tell her what I had experienced. When someone is hurting, they do not need to hear, "Let me tell you about my experience." Providentially, I was teaching this Bible study on Esther, so I sent her "Embracing God's Providence," the commentary from Lesson 1. She found great comfort in God's words. He had prepared me in advance to share with her in her time of need.

Losing a child involves a lifetime of unexpected and sudden sadness that accompanies his missed presence at special times and occasions. She is trusting God as she learns how to live by faith in his providence and goodness.

Where do you need courage to serve God on behalf of others? Are you facing the death of a loved one with both reality and courage? Are you seeking victory over a long-standing sin habit? If you die to your desire for this habit, which you must, you will find true life—life lived in the presence of and by the power of God. Face the facts and count the cost with courage; you will experience God personally in a way that is impossible otherwise. God sees all, knows all, has all power to work on your behalf, and will accomplish his purpose through you. However, if you refuse, he will give the blessing to another.

Esther was the mediator for her people before the king. Who is your mediator before God? Jesus Christ fully identified with his people, came to live among them, and laid down his life for them on the cross. He alone is qualified to be the mediator between our holy God and sinful people (John 14:6; 1 Timothy 2:5).

Through faith in Jesus as your Savior, you have been summoned into the very presence of God Almighty. You may approach God as Father without fear through Jesus, the Way. You have continual access into God's presence only if you are in Christ. You need not fear that you will perish, for your sins have already been laid on Jesus; he has suffered God's justifiable wrath toward you in your place. There is every reason to fear God if you approach him in any way other than what he has prescribed. Nadab and Abihu were consumed by fire for presuming to come to God in a way he had not commanded (Leviticus 10:1–2). God is concerned for his people. He sovereignly works on their behalf sometimes through a person like you, who demonstrates courage and trust in the face of reality. May you prove him faithful as you face the chaos and confusion in your life or the life of another.

Closing Prayer

My Father in heaven, thank you for the access into your presence that has been won for me by the Lord Jesus Christ's sacrificial atonement. May I not try to come in any other way. When I am afraid, help me run into your loving arms. When I am faced with chaos and confusion, help me draw near to you for wisdom and courage. Please develop my faith in you through whatever comes into my life today, tomorrow, and in the future. Thank you, Lord Jesus, for interceding before the Father on my behalf. When I have no words to pray, you and your Spirit are pleading with the Father on my behalf. O God, give me courage for today and hope for tomorrow, that I may bring honor and glory to your name and the name of my Savior, the Lord Jesus Christ. Amen.

Two Simultaneous, Opposing Plans

And when the king saw Queen Esther standing in the court, she won favor in his sight, and he held out to Esther the golden scepter that was in his hand. Then Esther approached and touched the tip of the scepter. (Esther 5:2)

This idea pleased Haman, and he had the gallows made. (Esther 5:14)

Text

Esther 5

Truth

God providentially controls the battle between good and evil to accomplish his purposes.

Hymn: "We Rest on Thee"

"We rest on thee"—our shield and our defender!
We go not forth alone against the foe;
Strong in thy strength, safe in thy keeping tender,
"We rest on thee, and in thy name we go."

Yea, "in thy name," O Captain of salvation!
In thy dear name, all other names above:
Jesus our righteousness, our sure foundation,
Our Prince of glory and our King of love.

"We go" in faith, our own great weakness feeling,
And needing more each day thy grace to know:
Yet from our hearts a song of triumph pealing,
"We rest on thee, and in thy name we go."

"We rest on thee"—our shield and our defender!
Thine is the battle, thine shall be the praise
When passing through the gates of pearly splendor,
Victors—we rest with thee, through endless days.

—EDITH G. CHERRY, CA. 1895

Opening Prayer

Lord God Almighty, the sovereign ruler of heaven and earth, I approach you with reverence and awe. You alone are God. There is no other. You have extended your hand to me by the cross of Jesus Christ, your Son. Through him I may approach you to find strength and courage in time of need. You guide me into paths of righteousness and to places beside still waters. When the fires of life seem overwhelming, you promise your presence will sustain me. I can rest on you as my shield and defender. I do not go alone against the culture, impending disasters, or those with evil intent. Lord Jesus, you are the captain of my salvation. Though I often feel weak, I am driven to you and your grace. You are my shield and defender. Teach me, O mighty God, what it looks like to interact with the people in our pagan culture in your mighty power, by resting on you. Your ways are indeed mysterious, but they are right and powerful to accomplish your redemptive purposes for your glory. Amen.

Questions for Study and Discussion

A Measured Response to the King

▶ READ ESTHER 5:1–8

1. Describe Esther's approach to the king and his response.

2. "An edict written in the name of the king and sealed with the king's ring cannot be revoked" (8:8b; see also 3:12–14). What potential options and risks did Esther face in talking to the king about the edict written by Haman?

3. What power did she have available in this discussion?

4. What was Esther's first request, and what does it tell you about her character and approach to the king?

5. What do you discern about the king from his response?

6. What was Esther's second request as her guests enjoyed after-dinner wine, and what does it reveal about her plan for her people?

7. How would the king's accepting the invitation assure her he would do whatever she asked? (See also 7:2.)

Haman's Ego Boost

▶ READ ESTHER 5:9–14

8. Describe Haman's fluctuating emotions as he left the feast.

9. How did Haman boost his ego after being humiliated again by Mordecai's refusal to rise or tremble with fear before him?

10. What does the size of the gallows (50 cubits, which is roughly 75 feet or 23 meters) reveal about Haman's hatred of Mordecai?

11. Compare the advice he received from his wife and friends to examples of worldly advice given today.

12. Was their advice good for Haman? Give reasons for your answer from this chapter.

13. What do you learn from Haman about pride, desire for recognition, and anger?

14. In what ways are you tempted as he was, and what are the dangers if you yield to the temptation?

15. Which words from "We Rest on Thee" or "God Moves in a Mysterious Way" (Lesson 2) help you in your approach to God in light of this chapter?

16. Write a prayer, approaching God with humility and respect, and ask him to help you apply these truths to your life.

Commentary

According to Jesus, two roads in life with different eternal destinations are before each of us (Matthew 7:13–14). Will we choose the righteous narrow road that leads to life? Or will we choose the evil broad road that leads to destruction and death? Will we glorify God, or will we seek ways to exalt ourselves? Will we run to God for salvation, or will we ignore him or even shake our fists at him in anger? Most of our choices are not a matter of life or death, God's way or sin, a godly choice or an ungodly choice, or even a wise choice and a foolish choice. In those cases, God has given us freedom to choose. However, this is not the kind of choice that Esther and Mordecai faced. Their situation was a matter of eternal significance for them and their people.

The Bible clearly teaches that God's way of salvation leads to God's blessing and any other way ultimately leads to God's wrath. That is not a popular message today, but it is true. God's people find hope in the truth that God's wrath they deserve was poured out on Christ, and that the battle between good and evil is under God's sovereign control. God remains faithful to his promises and purposes even when we do not. He uses people like Esther and Mordecai even if they are only nominally seeking his will and honor. He even uses the evil plans of people like Haman to accomplish his great purposes.

Chapter 5 records two human plans set in motion simultaneously, both in line with God's providence and purpose. Mordecai with loyalty and courage revealed his identity at great risk to himself and his people. Esther with humility and respect risked her life for the sake of her people, the Jews. Haman with arrogance and revenge sought to destroy those same people. He actually put himself against God. But they were God's covenant people, and no one could stop his covenantal purposes for them, not even the most honored and powerful man in the Persian kingdom. God would remain faithful to his covenant. The conflict between these two plans was under God's sovereign control. God would let Haman proceed only as far as he served God's purposes.

Mordecai and Esther's Plan (5:1–8)

Esther promised Mordecai that after three days of fasting she would approach the king, saying, "If I perish, I perish" (4:16). She could be deposed, just like her predecessor, Vashti. She could be executed. In spite of the danger, Esther set her plan in motion. She would need to please the king, submit to his authority, and build up his curiosity. She would need to expose the plight of the Jews and discredit Haman.

Approaching the King (5:1–2)

The first step was to approach the king according to court etiquette. Dressed in her royal robes, she entered the inner court of the king's palace in front of his quarters. He was seated on his throne opposite this entrance. Imagine the tension that must have been within her as she waited for him to see her. What would happen as he looked up and saw her?

The one good thing that could happen did. She found favor with the king, and he extended his golden scepter, an invitation to approach him. She humbly touched the tip of the scepter. Esther would not perish. Yet the edict remained. How could she and her people escape the scheduled genocide?

Esther's First Request (5:3–5)

The king may have sensed something big was troubling her. Why else would she risk coming to him without a summons? He asked, "What is it, Queen Esther? What is your request? It shall be given you, even to the half of my kingdom" (5:3). Was this simply a culturally grand gesture? Or did he mean she could ask him something big—including asking to reverse the edict sponsored by Haman that would annihilate her people? Imagine what incurring the wrath of Haman might mean. After all, he was the most powerful man in the empire, second only to the king. To reverse his edict would certainly cause an explosion from him. Besides, like changing an irrevocable trust today, it was legally impossible to revoke an edict written in the king's name and sealed with his ring (8:8). To break the law might cause the king to lose his credibility with his people—not a pleasant thought for him. Certainly she would have to reveal to him her secret of five years: "I am a Jew." How would he respond? How would he be able to show her favor?

Esther needed divine intervention on her behalf. Though queen, she had no miraculous power against Ahasuerus as Moses had against Pharaoh (Exodus 7–12) or Elijah against the prophets of Baal (1 Kings 18). Presumably she had discerned her strategy through the time of fasting. God does not always work in visibly miraculous ways to deliver his people. He sovereignly works through their personalities, gifts, and circumstances. He would work through Esther without a brilliant cloud, fire from heaven, or other spectacular intervention.

Appealing to the king's pleasure, Esther stated her request (5:4). She invited the king and Haman to a feast that she had already prepared. There was no time to waste. The food was ready. Was the king hungry? Was his curiosity aroused by her simple request or by her invitation to include Haman? The king accepted her invitation and gave orders to bring Haman quickly as Esther requested. Esther had a plan that would be unfolded carefully, not impulsively. She was setting up Haman for the unveiling of his evil by appealing to his arrogance and sense of his own importance.

Esther's Second Request (5:6–8)

Sipping after-dinner wine, the king surmised there was something more than this feast on Esther's mind. A second time he asked her, "What is your wish? It shall be granted you. And what is your request? Even to the half of my kingdom, it shall be fulfilled" (5:6). Esther did not rush; she showed patience, wisdom, and discernment as she waited for the right moment to expose Haman and for Haman to "hang himself."

Esther's second request was like the first. The king must have been surprised that Esther invited him and Haman to another feast the next day. She patiently waited for the right moment when the king was most receptive and Haman most vulnerable. She set the scene, so the king would have no alternative but to give her whatever she asked. She showed humble respect, saying, "If I have found favor . . . if it please the king . . . let the king . . . " (5:8). She acknowledged the king's authority and did not force her hand to take control. Finally, she promised to answer the king's request at the second feast. Actually, accepting her invitation would be tantamount to granting whatever she asked; not to do so would mean losing face by going back on a public promise that he had already given two times and would repeat another time (5:3, 6; 7:2).

Esther acted with respect and humility in her approach to the king. He appreciated these traits in his queen. Although her presence as the queen might be seen as a compromise of her Jewish heritage, she respected the person who had authority over her life in Persia. Her example illustrates a truth that God's people are wise to follow.

Truth: God Honors the Respectful and Humble

The Lord Jesus Christ humbled himself, respecting and desiring his Father's will throughout his earthly life, even to the point of his substitutionary atonement on the cross. He told his disciples, "My food [satisfaction, strength] is to do the will of him who sent me and to accomplish his work" (John 4:34). God honored him with a name that is above every name (Philippians 2:1–11) and with all authority in heaven and on earth (Matthew 28:18). Christ accomplished the work the Father gave him to do, providing us access to the throne of grace through his blood shed on the cross (Hebrews 4:16; 10:19–23). Through Christ we come to the God of love and grace, assured that he hears our requests and promises to answer them for his glory and our eternal good (Matthew 7:7). We do not come with fear and trembling, for Christ has taken the judgment for our sin upon himself. We who are in Christ come to our heavenly Father, the Father of our Lord Jesus Christ, as a young child trustingly runs to the open arms of his father and crawls into his lap.

In light of all God has done for you in Christ, how much are you willing to risk working for God on behalf of others? He has authority to ask you to risk your life, even to sacrifice your right to your life dreams and goals, to embrace his purposes for you (Romans 12:1). How does Christ's perfect life and finished work encourage you to approach God with respect, humility, and confident trust? How are you doing so? What is your attitude when approaching others who have authority over you?

God has not asked me to risk my life, but one time I had to face the uncertainty of losing my job and not knowing what the future would hold.

God unexpectedly closed a door in my career as a mathematics teacher. On Friday afternoon, I resigned my position when the college dean asked me to do something I considered unethical, that violated my integrity. When I got home, I told my husband, Jim, I was no longer employed. He looked surprised but commented, "Don't worry. Remember, we decided to live on my salary when we got married. We will just have to cut out some extra things."

174

I spent a lot of that night pondering what this would mean for us and for my career. The next morning, Jim was attending a class at our alma mater, Texas State University. As he walked across the campus, he met my former professor Dr. Burrell Helton, who inquired about me and my job. This was the first and only time he encountered Dr. Helton on the campus that summer. Jim told him I had just resigned. By God's providential grace, Dr. Helton told Jim that if I was interested in a faculty position at TSU in their mathematics department, I should call him Monday morning and it would be mine! I taught there for three years before deciding to stay home when our daughter, Kristin, was born. The following year I was asked to be a group leader in Bible Study Fellowship. The day after I said yes, I was given the opportunity to take a position at Texas Lutheran University in their mathematics department. A day before, I would have taken the job without giving it much thought. By God's providence, I remembered something my parents had taught me: "If you have agreed to do something, you must keep your word, even if something 'better' comes along." My integrity was being tested again. I knew I would be a BSF leader when class began in a few weeks. Little did I know at the time that God was preparing me to teach the Bible, train Bible teachers, and prepare Bible study materials for BSF on into "retirement."

Haman's Plan (5:9–14)

Haman's Fluctuating Emotions (5:9–10a)

Not knowing Esther's plan, Haman formulated a plan of his own. The arrogant Haman had evil designs fed by his ego and desire to be exalted by everyone in the kingdom. Imagine

Haman walking away from the feast, high from wine and elated over his prestigious position. He could see everyone rising up and bowing down before him.

But Haman's happiness turned to rage at the sight of Mordecai sitting in the king's gate. As usual, Mordecai neither rose nor trembled before Haman. Haman could not bear the humiliation. He was powerless to make Mordecai fear or respect him. Worse than that, everyone could see Mordecai's disrespect. Haman was filled with wrath, the fruit of the revenge and bitterness boiling inside him. He must deal with Mordecai before he could enjoy the second feast. In spite of his boiling anger, he did not take immediate action.

Haman's Helpers (5:10b–14a)

Haman held a party at his home, looking to his wife and friends for comfort. He presented a long, detailed narrative of his grand résumé, which all of them probably knew already. He recounted the splendor of his riches, the number of his sons, and his promotions over all officials and servants—clear indications of his power. He added another point they may not have known. He alone had been invited to Esther's feast that she prepared for the king. Furthermore, he was the only other guest invited to the feast for the next day. While it seemed he had both the king and queen in the palm of his hand, he was actually setting himself up for destruction (Proverbs 16:18). He was not considering God's providence bringing all these details together.

What more could he desire? He must have the one thing he could not legislate—Mordecai bowing before him! His boasting turned to whining as he explained that all this fame meant nothing because Mordecai the Jew sat at the king's gate and refused to bow before him.

His wife and friends came to his rescue. Their advice was similar to what one hears in our day: "Vent! You have a right to feel anger toward him. Get rid of him no matter what you have to do! You deserve better treatment in light of your importance. Make him pay. Don't get mad, get even." Their plan was like music to his ears: "Let a gallows 50 cubits [75 feet or 23 meters] high be made, and in the morning tell the king to have Mordecai hanged upon it" (5:14). The enormous height reflected the magnitude of Haman's rage. It was not enough to kill Mordecai; all must see him on the gallows. Hanging on a gallows today means being hanged by the neck. The *NIV Archaeological Study Bible* says, "Pictures and statues from the ancient Near East and the comments of the historian Herodotus (2.125, 129; 4:43) confirm that the Persian practice of 'hanging' was actually impalement. . . . In Israelite and Canaanite practice, hanging was an exhibition of the corpse and not the means of execution itself."[1] How interesting that they advised him to go to the palace early in the morning so he could tell the king to hang Mordecai on the gallows. Was Haman now giving orders to the king? How would you have advised Haman?

Haman's Defining Moment (5:14b)

Thrilled with their idea, Haman had the gallows built immediately. They must be ready so that he could tell the king to have Mordecai hanged first thing in the morning. Then, and only then, he would be able to go joyfully with the king to Esther's feast. Alas for Haman! He would find that working against God's people is actually working against God. It would be a dead-end road leading to his death. We learn an important truth as we look at Haman:

---

1. Study note on Esther 2:23 in the *NIV Archaeological Study Bible* (Grand Rapids: Zondervan, 2005).

Truth: God Lets the Revengeful and Prideful Self-Destruct

This truth is explained in Romans 1:18–32. Ultimately, God will not let revenge and pride stand against him or his people. Haman could not imagine that tanyone else was worthy of praise. His whole world revolved around himself, even at the expense of others. Arrogance and self-promotion prohibited him from right thinking. His pride and quest for power outweighed his respect for human life and the rights of others. His hatred for the Jews and Mordecai progressed to revenge and bitterness that knew no restraint. He would be satisfied with nothing less than the annihilation of Mordecai and the Jews. Mordecai challenged Haman's self-worship. He must get rid of Mordecai. He could not wait until the month of Adar. It had to be immediately. Nothing else mattered. God was sovereignly at work even in Haman's rush to build the gallows. Haman did not realize that these gallows would be the means to his own death.

Where are you in danger of being arrogant and hungry for power or prestige? Who stands in your way, and to what ends will you go to get rid of him, her, or them? What ideas, beliefs, tasks, or things consume your thoughts, time, and energy? How are they being challenged, and what emotions do these challenges arouse in you? How are these challenges opportunities to turn to Christ, the only One who satisfies your need for fulfillment, joy, and meaning in life?

Mounting Tension

The tension mounted as Mordecai's fate was now in the hands of the king. Whose influence would prevail—Esther's or Haman's? Would Esther's humility and respect win out over Haman's pride and revenge? On the one hand, Queen Esther, after fasting (and perhaps praying) for three days, humbly approached the king and received his favor. He honored her with his company at the banquet where they cordially drank wine together (5:1–8). On the other hand, Haman moved from celebratory drinking with the king (3:15; 5:6) to rage and premeditated murder of Mordecai (5:9–14). Would Esther's loyalty to the king and favor with him give her the advantage over Haman? Would Haman's abusive power become his downfall? Would God's providence prevail?

As the narrative unfolds, seemingly insignificant and forgotten details come to the forefront. God's plan for his people initiated through Esther would prevail against the evil plans of Haman. Mordecai's steadfast refusal to bow to Haman would push Haman to the limit of his tolerance. He could wait no longer to get rid of Mordecai. The counsel of Haman's wife and friends led him to build the massive gallows that would carry out his own death sentence. This, too, was part of God's sovereign plan to save his people from genocide in Persia. Iain Duguid writes,

> God's sovereignty operates in such a way that our freedom and responsibility to act are not compromised, yet the end result is still exactly what God has purposed from the beginning. Just as Esther, Mordecai, Haman, and Ahasuerus were not compelled to act contrary to their wills, but still did exactly what God had planned, so too we are never mere robots, yet we see God accomplishing his purposes in and through us. . . . What is more, God achieves his perfect goals not just through our best intentions and most self-sacrificing acts, but even through our greatest sins and compromises.[2]

---

2. Iain M. Duguid, *Esther and Ruth*, Reformed Expository Commentary (Phillipsburg, NJ: P&R Publishing, 2005), 69.

It is utmost folly to oppose God. Psalm 14:1 says, "The fool says in his heart, 'There is no God.'" Other renderings of this verse are, "The fool says in his heart, 'No, God!'" or, "No God!" Whether one shakes his fist at God or denies the existence of God, his refusal is the epitome of folly. Those who attempt to thwart God's plan actually become his instruments to accomplish it. Why were Mordecai and Esther in Persia? It is beginning to be clear that they were there for God's deliverance of the Jews. He would accomplish his purposes in and through them, Ahasuerus, and even Haman.

God sovereignly controls the battle between good and evil. The end was revealed at the cross of Jesus Christ. His death defeated the Devil and death. God providentially controlled each step to the final victory. His purposes will always prevail because he alone is God; there is no other.

Closing Prayer

Lord God Almighty, seeing your providence in the narrative of Esther, I am amazed and thrilled at what I learn about you. Wicked people like Haman do not surprise you. Neither are you dismayed by their arrogance and sense of entitlement. You reward the humble and respectful, entrusting your imperfect people with great responsibility in your kingdom. You let the proud and revengeful self-destruct. I worship you for your sovereignty, wisdom, love, and power. You control the battle between good and evil. The victory was made certain by the death and resurrection of Jesus. You providentially control each of my steps to the realized victory. May I approach you with humility and respect before I ask for anything from your gracious hand. Then may I go forward in faith, resting on you, the sovereign God who rules and reigns forever and ever, who is also my heavenly Father. Amen.

Haman's Obituary: Honor, Humiliation, and Hanging

On that night the king could not sleep. (Esther 6:1)

Text

Esther 6–7

Truth

God writes our biographies in accord with his divine sovereignty and our human responsibility.

Hymn: "The Lord Has Heard and Answered Prayer"

The Lord has heard and answered prayer
And saved His people in distress;
This to the coming age declare,
That they His holy name may bless.

The Lord, exalted on His throne,
Looked down from Heav'n with pitying eye
To still the lowly captive's moan
And save His people doomed to die.

All men in Zion shall declare
His gracious name with one accord,
When kings and nations gather there
To serve and worship God the Lord.

The earth and heav'ns shall pass away,
Like vesture worn and laid aside,
But changeless Thou shalt live for aye,
Thy years forever shall abide.

Thou, O Jehovah, shalt endure;
Thy throne forever is the same;
And to all generations sure
Shall be Thy great memorial name.

—*The Psalter*, 1912 (PSALM 102:17–27)

Opening Prayer

Sovereign God of all power and might, how beautiful it is to watch your providence unfold in your Word and in my life. You are sovereign even over sleepless nights, through evil plots against your people, and in timely entrances and exits. Please teach me once again of your sovereignty and my responsibility. Help me to be faithful to trust you and to hear you speak through your Word this day. For the glory of your name, my great God and King. Amen.

Questions for Study and Discussion

The Plot Twists, and Turns, on Haman

▶ READ ESTHER 6:1–10

1. What part did the king's insomnia play in God's protection of his people, the Jews?

2. How might your sleepless nights play a part in God's overarching plan of redemption for yourself or another?

3. What do you learn about Haman from his approach to the king and his response to the king?

4. Try to describe Haman's inner turmoil when he heard the king say, "Hurry . . . do [what you have said] to Mordecai. . . . Leave out nothing" (v. 10).

5. What lessons do you learn about God's power over the plans of evil people?

6. Where are you tempted to show revenge to one who annoys or hurts you, and what might you expect from God if you leave revenge to him?

A Chastened Haman

▶ READ ESTHER 6:11–14

7. How did the king's edict demolish Haman's ego?

8. Compare the advice of Haman's wife and friends with what they had told him previously. (See 5:13–14.)

9. What truth about God's protection of his people can you draw from their advice?

Esther's Second Feast

▶ READ ESTHER 7:1–10

10. How did Esther show wisdom, integrity, and humility at the second feast? (See also 5:8.)

11. Do you think Esther knew about Mordecai's parade of honor? Give reasons for your answer from chapters 6 and 7.

12. What dilemma did the king now face?

13. Explain Haman's plan to try to escape.

14. What connecting words in verse 8 show the split-second timing of events in chapter 7?

God Was in Control All Along

▶ REVIEW ESTHER 6–7

15. What truths about God's people and God's plan do you learn from chapters 6–7?

16. What has God asked you to do that will require you to risk yourself, and how does this chapter help you obey him?

17. Write a prayer that includes adoration of God's sovereign power, thanksgiving for God's past faithfulness to protect you, and a request for God to help you risk all to obey him.

Commentary

Have you ever found it difficult or even impossible to fall asleep? Your mind races through events of the day or plans for tomorrow. Nothing you do seems to stop your brain activity. Could your sleeplessness be God's way of keeping you awake because he is doing something significant in your life?

We left Haman plotting to hang Mordecai. He thought he could eliminate his problems by removing Mordecai. It seemed Esther might be too late to save her cousin even though she might be able to save the Jews and herself. However, God was providentially active to save his people. It was not Mordecai who was in grave danger. The stage was being set for Haman's demise.

How interesting that the king's sleepless night turned around the life of another and an entire kingdom. This was not "coincidence," "fate," or "luck." God sovereignly used the ordinary details of life to accomplish his purposes and save his people. Nevertheless, God's sovereignty in history did not negate human responsibility. Esther was responsible to plan her way: "The heart of man plans his way, but the LORD establishes his steps" (Proverbs 16:9). "Unless the LORD builds the house, those who build it labor in vain" (Psalm 127:1a). Another truth played out in Haman's life: presuming to stop God's plan by attempting to destroy his people is sheer folly. It will ultimately result in utter defeat and death. God's plan will not be thwarted by evil. Also, God holds us responsible for our choices. Haman went from honor to humiliation to hanging. God is also writing our biographies according to both his divine sovereignty and our human responsibility.

Haman's Desire for Honor (6:1–10)

The King's Insomnia (6:1–4a)

In spite of having had a full day, the king could not sleep. The text gives no reason such as illness, war, or a major decision. His insomnia in light of the other events points to God's providence. Because he could not sleep, he asked to have the book of memorable deeds read to him. This reveals something about the king: if he cannot sleep, he wants to hear about his triumphs.

Who opened the book to just the right page that he would hear about Mordecai's part in saving his life by reporting the conspiracy of his eunuchs, Bigthana and Teresh (2:19–23)? This could hardly be considered "chance." Mordecai's act of loyal valor in exposing the conspiracy had occurred about five years earlier. But Mordecai had not been publicly acknowledged and rewarded. Something needed to be done immediately. The king might have become fearful that no one would protect him in the future if rewards were omitted. Seeking the help of his counselors, he asked his servants, "Who is in the court?" (6:4). Remember, this is early morning.

Split-Second Timing (6:4b–6)

Just at that moment, Haman entered the outer court to speak to the king about hanging Mordecai. He needed the king's approval to get rid of Mordecai. We cannot escape God's providence in the "little" things in this split-second timing. The king gave Haman permission to enter and, before Haman could say a word, the king posed the big question: "What should be done to the man whom the king delights to honor?" (6:6). How ironic he did not name the man to be honored, just as Haman had not named the Jews in his plot to destroy them (3:8). Neither Haman nor the king knew the significance of this question. God was writing their biographies through this interaction. Haman was so certain the king wanted to honor him that he omitted the normal courteous address, "If it please the king." He immediately described what he wanted for himself. Never did he imagine the king was planning to honor anyone but him, least of all Mordecai.

Haman's Plan (6:7–10)

Haman explained his self-serving plan to honor "someone." One of the king's most noble officials was to dress him in the king's clothes and crown, then lead him on the king's horse through the city square, proclaiming, "Thus shall it be done to the man whom the king delights to honor" (6:9).

The king liked the idea so much he told Haman to implement it immediately. What a blow to Haman and his exalted opinion of himself! Instead of receiving the king's permission to hang Mordecai, Haman would honor Mordecai, leaving out no detail of the plan he had laid out before the king. Could there have been anything worse? Imagine Haman's spiking blood pressure, racing heartbeat, and shortened breath as he realized all his plans to do evil to Mordecai suddenly turned upon him. He had no option but to obey the king. Inside he was seething like a volcano ready to erupt. Yet he had to appear calm on the outside.

Do you see what God can do when you leave revenge to him? The surprising turn of events clearly reveals God's hand in the lives of Esther, Mordecai, Haman, Ahasuerus, and the Jews.

Truth: God Is Sovereign over Details

No detail escapes God's notice. Sleepless nights are opportunities to pray for a person or situation that comes to mind. I have knelt beside the bed of my sleeping children or grandchildren to pray for their salvation or problems they are facing.

Do you question God's providence in the "little" things of your life—interruptions, cancellations, a person in need, a closed door? How might your "little thing" be evidence of God's providence and something of eternal significance for you or others? How might God use it for your spiritual growth or preparation to bless you and use you to bless others?

Do you doubt God controls the affairs of men? How does the turn of events for Mordecai and Haman give you hope that God turns the plans of evil people to accomplish his good purposes for you, your family, your church, your nation, and the world

(Romans 8:28–29)? Ask him to open your eyes to see how his providence has brought you to this moment.

Why does God not always immediately turn the evil plans upon evil perpetrators? Why does he allow evil to happen to his people? "How long?" is a question frequently asked by God's people in difficult times. There is no simple answer. But this I know for a fact: God shelters his people in the midst of evil. Read the stories of martyrs who were burned at the stake or tossed to hungry lions for believing the gospel of Jesus Christ. They had peace that passes understanding because God put his sheltering grace around them even as they died. We are not called to escape suffering. Evil is perpetrated against God's people, but nothing touches his people without his permission. He will not allow suffering to last even a second longer than necessary to accomplish his purposes in it. He knows what is best for our eternal good and for the accomplishment of his plan. Sometimes others are watching and are drawn to the Savior by his people's steadfast faith in God demonstrated in the face of suffering.

Does God ordain evil for the eternal good of his elect people? The answer is yes. The ultimate example is the cross of Jesus Christ, God's planned event from eternity past that was carried out by the evil actions of people. Job suffered because God drew Satan's attention to Job, initiating the sequence of disasters that struck him (Job 1–2). God set limits on what Satan could do. When Job lamented his birth, God allowed Job's "friends" to add more pain by their half-truths and accusations (Job 3–37). Finally, God himself gave Job a test (38:1-40:34) for which Job could only answer, "I don't know" (40:3–5). In the end, Job responded with joyful submission to God's power and purposes (42:1–6). Without being evil himself, God not only allows evil but also ordains it to display his power and accomplish his purposes and plan.

Haman's Humiliation (6:11–14)

Haman's Humiliation (6:11)

Haman was forced to honor Mordecai as the king commanded. Imagine Haman's controlled rage as he led Mordecai through the city, proclaiming, "Thus shall it be done to the man whom the king delights to honor" (6:11). All would see the honor Mordecai, not Haman, received.

Mordecai's Humility (6:12)

Mordecai returned to the king's gate. Apparently, he was not impressed with the parade and the honor given him. He was probably thinking about Esther's winning the king's favor. In contrast, humiliated Haman covered his head and rushed home mourning. Instead of public recognition, he experienced public humiliation. Again he turned to those who would stroke his wounded ego. He told them everything, perhaps saying, "You won't believe what just happened to me."

God's Providence in Haman's Humiliation (6:13–14)

Even the counsel of his "wise" friends and wife had changed. Previously, they told him the abiding principle of the world, "Get rid of Mordecai if he stands in your way." Now they advised, "If Mordecai, before whom you have begun to fall, is of the Jewish people, you will not overcome him but will surely fall before him" (6:13). They were beyond thinking the events were mere coincidence. Without knowing it, they were speaking truth from God: if God's purpose for his people gets in your way, you will not win by fighting God. Neither can God's purpose for you fail, as you trust him. Tragically, Haman did not recognize these great truths and repent. Time was running out for him.

Once again we see the split-second timing of God's providence: "While they were yet talking with him, the king's eunuchs arrived and hurried to bring Haman to the feast that Esther had prepared" (6:14).

Truth: God Holds People Responsible for Their Actions

Haman was responsible for what happened to him. God would not ignore Haman's fighting against him and his people. Neither will he ignore your challenges to his truth and dishonoring of his people.

Are you trying to silence someone who challenges your view of God by her life or words? I have been told, "I happen to like my Jesus because he is love and never tells me I've done wrong. He always says yes to my prayers." Such wrong thinking about God will not go unnoticed. Instead of embracing "another Jesus," what if this person asked, "How can I live in a way that honors you, God?" He might reveal through his Word that she should stop believing in "that Jesus" and start believing in the true Jesus. Jesus said, "I am the way, and the truth, and the life. No one comes to the Father except through me" (John 14:6). On what are you building your life—your own ideas of importance, the world's standards of success, or God's gracious provision of Jesus Christ? God holds you responsible for what he has taught you in his Word, how you treat other people, and how you treat his Son, Jesus. Some want to have Jesus as Savior but continue to handle the details of their lives by themselves. You cannot have Jesus as Savior and not as Lord. He is both or neither in your life.

Paul said knowing Christ was more important to him than anything else. His purpose was striving toward the finish line (Philippians 3:8–14). If you are Christ's, he has made you his own to press on to be like him. You may feel that you have failed, but failure does not take you out of Christ. God helps you press beyond failure toward your goal of becoming like Christ.

If you resist God and insist on your way, you could come crashing down just as quickly as Haman did. Haman's humiliation could have turned him toward humility, crying out to God for mercy, but it did not. However, you have time to turn to the Lord Jesus Christ for satisfaction and salvation. Will you?

Haman's Hanging (7:1–10)

Esther's Second Feast (7:1)

Haman may have thought things could not get worse, but he was about to find out they could and would. He and the king went in to the feast Esther had prepared for them. Somehow the joy Haman had the previous day was dimmed by the public humiliation and gloomy private prediction he had received.

Esther's Request (7:2–4)

Drinking wine after the feast, the king again asked Esther, "What is your wish, Queen Esther? It shall be granted you. And what is your request? Even to the half of my kingdom, it shall be fulfilled" (7:2). Did Esther know about Haman's parade of Mordecai? We are not told, but it would be surprising if her maids and eunuchs had not mentioned it to her. In any case, she realized the time to act was now. Showing integrity, she did as promised the day before. She told the king what was on her mind.

With respect for the king, she humbly said, "If I have found favor in your sight, O king, and if it please the king, let my life be granted me for my wish, and my people for my request"

200

(7:3). She included both parts of his promise—her wish and her request—explaining, "We have been sold, I and my people" (7:4). She wisely did not give too much information but left room for him to question, "What? How? By whom?" Carefully and strategically, she added more details: "to be destroyed, to be killed, and to be annihilated." I wonder if the king was asking, "Why? When?" Esther did not tell him everything at once. Are you wise enough to give people time to ask questions before you give them the answers?

Quickly she added another layer, "If we had been sold merely as slaves, men and women, I would have been silent, for our affliction is not to be compared with the loss to the king" (7:4). Finally, she appealed to his self-interest. He could benefit from enslaving them but not from killing them.

Haman's Unmasking (7:5–6)

Esther had ignited the fire of the king's anger and had his rapt attention. He asked, "Who is he, and where is he, who has dared to do this?" (7:5). Can you imagine Haman's thoughts? Esther's strategy and demeanor outwitted him. Mordecai had humbled him; now the queen had trapped him. Esther turned to Haman and revealed him as he was, "A foe and enemy! This wicked Haman!" (7:6). Haman was justifiably terrified before the king and queen.

Ahasuerus's Rage (7:7a)

The final piece of the puzzle of Haman's humiliation was the king's response. Providentially rising in his wrath, the king went into the garden. The king's top man in the empire is trying to kill the queen, but the king was probably more concerned about his own reputation than what happened to Haman. How

201

could he, without losing face, punish Haman and undo Haman's edict he had approved?

Haman's Folly (7:7b–8a)

As the king pondered his dilemma, Haman stayed inside to beg Esther for his life. She was his last resort. He discerned the harm the king intended for him. What irony that he begged Esther to save his life when he had planned to kill her and all her people. With split-second timing, the king returned to see Haman "falling on the couch where Esther was" (7:8). How foolish of Haman to be in such a compromising position. Not only was he alone with the queen, but he was also giving the appearance of assaulting her. The *NIV Archaeological Study Bible* says, "Protocol dictated that no one but the king could be left alone with a woman of the royal harem. . . . Once the king had exited, Haman should have left Esther's presence. That he moved onto her couch was unthinkable!"[1] The king now had a reason to get rid of Haman.

Haman's Death Sentence (7:8b–10)

Aghast, the king exclaimed, "Will he even assault the queen in my presence, in my own house?" (7:8). The italicized words below point to the providential outworking of God's plan for Esther, Mordecai, the Jews, and Haman. *As* the word left the king's mouth, "they covered Haman's face." He was already as good as dead. *Then* Harbona, one of the king's eunuchs, *just happened* to offer another important bit of information for the king. "*Moreover*, the gallows that Haman has prepared for Mordecai,

---

1. Study note on Esther 7:7–8 in the *NIV Archaeological Study Bible* (Grand Rapids: Zondervan, 2005).

whose word saved the king, is standing at Haman's house" (7:9). The king quickly replied, "Hang him on that" (7:10).

Haman's honor turned to humiliation, then hanging. His obituary was short: "So they hanged Haman on the gallows that he had prepared for Mordecai. Then the wrath of the king abated" (7:10).

Truth: God Is Always on Time—Never Early and Never Late

If Esther had moved too quickly in exposing Haman, the providential timing of the king's sleeplessness would have been thrown off. Mordecai would have had no special place of honor in the king's mind. The gallows would not have been ready for Haman. Only God could write and direct such a drama.

Esther risked her life to save her people, and Haman was removed. Yet Haman's irrevocable edict still stood. What could she do to counteract it? How would God providentially work for his people now? God was always providentially writing the script for each member of the cast. His faithfulness did not depend on theirs. God moved in mysterious ways his wonders to perform.

God's sovereign act in the king's sleeplessness was the turning point of the book of Esther. Yet God also worked through the faithful plans of Esther and Mordecai. He providentially accomplished his purposes through his people and through the seemingly ordinary details of life. Their plans could only come to pass through God's divine intervention and providence. He was writing their biographies.

He is also the author of our biographies. We do not write our stories. We live out the biography God has written for us in accordance with his plan and purposes. He includes chapters we probably would not have written: terminal illness of yourself or a loved one; rebellion of a child; struggles in the family or church; threats and actions of terrorists. Looking back, we are able to see how they have shaped us and taught us to trust God in ways we might never have done without them.

Where do you need God to work on your behalf—marriage, family, workplace, church, nation? Will you approach your situation with prayer and action? Will you do what you can as the Lord leads while also trusting in him to do what only he can do?

How do you know what God is telling you? You read his Word. Answer the hard questions in this study. Be honest with yourself. You cannot change another person; only God can change the heart. What you can do is change yourself with God's help and love the other person, trusting God to change him or her. You may discover that you cannot change some circumstances. You may never see any difference in people around you or in your circumstances, but you will find joy and peace as God transforms you. Be committed to God and his desires for you in the place where he has put you right now. You will be content no matter what happens.

Do you recognize the providential hand of God in your life? How have you seen his split-second timing in the details of your life? How does this encourage you to trust God? Carole's Bible study prepared her to recognize God's providence in a very specific situation that has brought her and her husband, Johnny, great peace and joy.

Through my Bible study in recent months, God has been revealing to me his perfect sovereignty over my life and those I love. He has convinced me that it is not "apart from" but rather "a part of" his grace to which I have clung so long. Johnny and I were confronted with his need for a full hip replacement. We both developed a vague uneasiness about the current practices and circumstances as we went through the diagnostic and early treatment phase with our trusted orthopedic group. Over the past two years, Johnny has had critical complications from a "minor" elective surgery done by one of the outstanding general surgeons in our area. The reality of potential critical complications for Johnny's hip replacement convinced us that we needed to seek first God's opinion and then a second orthopedic opinion regarding who should perform the required operation. Then we needed to be sensitive to God's response!

The next morning, right after we prayed for God's guidance, we received an email from a Christian personal friend and business leader at Johnny's workplace. This was totally unexpected. She literally asked us to seek a second opinion, opinion, saying "I don't want John to have such trouble as the last time." We immediately saw this as God's answer to our prayer. As we proceeded to explore the surgeon she suggested, not an encounter went by but that God confirmed in even minute details that he was choosing not only this man but also his entire group and the hospital as well. As we approach the surgical date and are made aware of the many details needed for a successful outcome, we have been strengthened in two truths I learned in studying Esther: God's providence provides a way to discern his will in specific situations, and faith in God's providence produces joy as we see our lives and the lives of others unfold under God's direction. Though we do not know what may unfold over the next weeks or months, we are certain that we are where God wants us to be. The truth of Isaiah 42:16 will remind us as we go:

205

And I will lead the blind
in a way that they do not know,
in paths that they have not known
I will guide them.
I will turn the darkness before them into light,
the rough places into level ground.
These are the things I do,
and I do not forsake them.

The surgery was successful and Johnny was released to go home the following day. God may protect him from complications for the praise of his glory. If some should arise, God will strengthen Johnny and Carole and guide them through the rough places. Either way, they are resting in God's providential care.

Haman's plot fell apart because he was working against God. He wanted to be honored by the king. "God opposes the proud but gives grace to the humble" (James 4:6). Who is the one God delights to honor? He delights to honor his Son, the Lord Jesus Christ. Peter proclaimed before three thousand people on the day of Pentecost, "Let all the house of Israel therefore know for certain that God has made him both Lord and Christ, this Jesus whom you crucified" (Acts 2:36). Paul wrote, "Therefore God has highly exalted him and bestowed on him the name that is above every name, so that at the name of Jesus every knee should bow, in heaven and on earth and under the earth, and every tongue confess that Jesus Christ is Lord, to the glory of God the Father" (Philippians 2:9–11). To resist honoring Jesus Christ is to go against God and his purpose for all people.

What is your attitude toward what God desires? How can

you honor Jesus Christ as Lord? How do your words and actions confess him as Lord? Perhaps you are resisting God or trying to get rid of his people and their influence on your thinking and life. God holds you responsible if you fail to confess and honor Jesus as Lord. God will oppose you and you will lose in the ultimate sense. It is never too late to turn to God in contrition and repentance. Will you today delight and honor God by receiving his gracious gift of the Lord Jesus? Today could be the beginning of a new chapter in your biography, whose author is God.

Closing Prayer

Lord God Almighty, sovereign ruler of all, you providentially order people, events, and time to accomplish your divine purpose. You write the script for my life according to your perfect will. Forgive me when I suggest "coincidence" or "luck" is behind the details of my life. Forgive me for being resentful when things seem to go poorly for me. Forgive me when I forget to thank you when things go well. Remind me of your providence through each detail of my life. Help me proclaim with courage and faithfulness your providence over every circumstance of my life. Truly, you move in mysterious ways your wonders to perform. Open my eyes to see the bitter bud of conviction of sin that is becoming the sweet flower of Jesus' life in me. Give me faith to trust you for your grace and your wise interpretation of the details of my life. For your glory. Amen.

Celebrating Deliverance of the Jews

Therefore they called these days Purim, after the term Pur. . . . The Jews firmly obligated themselves and their offspring and all who joined them, that without fail they would keep these two days . . . that these days should be remembered and kept throughout every generation . . . and that these days of Purim should never fall into disuse among the Jews, nor should the commemoration of these days cease among their descendants. (Esther 9:26–28)

Text

Esther 8–10

Truth

God's salvation and deliverance initiate a new life of gratitude, peace, and joy.

Hymn: "Loved with Everlasting Love"

Loved with everlasting love,
Led by grace that love to know,
Gracious Spirit from above,
Thou hast taught me it is so.
O this full and precious peace!
O this transport all divine!
In a love which cannot cease,
I am His and He is mine.

Heav'n above is softer blue,
Earth around is sweeter green!
Something lives in every hue
Christless eyes have never seen;
Birds with gladder songs o'erflow,
Flowers with deeper beauties shine,
Since I know, as now I know,
I am His and He is mine.

Things that once were wild alarms
Cannot now disturb my rest;
Closed in everlasting arms,
Pillowed on the loving breast.
O to lie forever here,
Doubt and care and self resign,
While He whispers in my ear,
I am His and He is mine.

His forever, only His;
Who the Lord and me shall part?

210

Ah, with what a rest of bliss
Christ can fill the loving heart!
Heav'n and earth may fade and flee,
Firstborn light in gloom decline;
But while God and I shall be,
I am His and He is mine.

—GEORGE W. ROBINSON, 1890

Opening Prayer

Gracious God, our Savior and Lord, I am filled with joy as I remember what the Lord Jesus Christ accomplished on my behalf as he died in my place. May I grow in gratitude and thanksgiving, not just for one day in the year but hour by hour and minute by minute. Show me how to be intentional in expressing my gratitude to you and to others. Thank you in advance for how you will direct my steps and put words on my lips. To you belong all honor and glory. Amen.

Questions for Study and Discussion

A New Appeal and Reward

▶ READ ESTHER 8:1–17

1. How were Esther and Mordecai rewarded?

2. Compare Esther's appeal to the king with her previous appeal in 5:1–8.

3. What seems significant to you about the king's response to this second appeal?

4. In what ways has God entrusted authority to you, and how does Mordecai's example help you assume that authority?

5. What was the message of Mordecai's edict?

6. Who has God-given authority over you? What do you learn from Esther and Mordecai about appealing to these authorities for the sake of God's people?

7. How do you see God's providence in the response to Mordecai's edict compared with the response to Haman's edict (4:1–3)?

Turned Tables

▶ READ ESTHER 9:1–10

8. What was the outcome of the planned destruction of the Jews?

9. Did the Jews completely follow the king's instructions given in Mordecai's edict? Why or why not?

The King's Continued Favor

▶ READ ESTHER 9:11–19

10. How had Esther progressed in favor with the king and in power in the kingdom?

11. What was Esther's request, and why did she ask it?

12. What happened to Israel when they did not completely destroy their enemies? See Joshua 13:1, 13; 15:63; 16:10; 23:11–13.

13. How and why has God provided for his people to persevere in destroying sinful habits and resisting temptation? See Ephesians 6:10–18; 1 Timothy 6:12; James 4:7; and 1 John 1:9.

The Celebration of Purim

▶ READ ESTHER 9:20–10:3

14. What is the Feast of Purim, and why was it established?

15. How have spontaneous celebrations turned into traditions in your life?

16. How did Mordecai's greatness compare with Haman's?

17. What commendable leadership qualities did Mordecai exhibit? How can you seek to emulate him in relating to those you lead in your home, workplace, church, or other places?

God's Working behind the Scenes

▶ REVIEW ESTHER 1–10

18. What is the most important, most personal lesson you have learned from the book of Esther?

19. What difference has it made in your beliefs, priorities, actions, and love for God and his people? Be specific.

Commentary

Does saying "thank you" to God come naturally for you? What about expressing thanks or gratitude to others? Is gratitude an obvious trait of your family or workplace or church? Having our eyes opened to see God's providence, grace, and goodness in fresh ways stirs our hearts to be grateful. The more we look for God's grace in daily provisions and in Christ, the more God's Spirit motivates us to be grateful. Intentional expressions of thanks to God and others deepen our understanding of the importance of gratitude, even for difficulties. Individual expressions of gratitude to God and to others are contagious.

Sometimes a spontaneous celebration of God's grace in salvation can become an annual tradition. This is what happened to Esther, Mordecai, and the Jews as they celebrated God's salvation for them in Persia. God's salvation involved favor with the king, joy for the Jews, destruction of their enemies, institution of an annual feast of celebration, and a place of honor for Mordecai. For the Jews, gratitude for their salvation was the road to joy. Did they deserve God's providential work in their favor? No, and neither do we. Recognizing the gracious hand of God in our salvation leads to gratitude, peace, and joy.

Salvation for the Jews (8:1–9:19)

Esther risked her life to save her people, saying, "If I perish, I perish" (4:16). However, it was clearly God's favor toward her and her people that saved her. The king invited her to enter his presence and tell him what was on her heart. He ordered Haman to honor Mordecai instead of himself. With wisdom and skill, Esther exposed Haman and his evil plot to kill her and her people. The king ordered Haman to be hanged on the very gallows he built to destroy Mordecai. Do you see the providential grace of God in these events leading up to this chapter?

Mordecai's Promotion (8:1–2)

God removed the evil Haman, but the edict to destroy Esther and her people was still in effect (8:8). However, Esther was in excellent standing with the king. He gave her the house of Haman on the very day that Haman was hanged. Up to this point, Esther had only told the king that she was a Jew condemned to death by the edict. Now she revealed her relationship to Mordecai, opening the way for him to approach the king. The king was feeling very generous toward Esther, so he gave Mordecai his signet ring that he had retrieved from Haman. Esther then honored Mordecai by setting him over the house of Haman that now belonged to her. From being slated for death, the king honored Esther and Mordecai above all others.

Esther's Plea (8:3–7)

Esther knew the law and court etiquette. She wasted no time in moving forward while she had the king's attention and favor. Falling at his feet and weeping, she pled with him to stop Haman's evil plan. As he extended his scepter to her, she again approached him with humility and respect: "If it please the king ... if I have found favor in his sight ... if the thing seems right before the king ... [if] I am pleasing in his eyes" (8:5). Would her request please him? Did she please him? Once again, she was putting her life on the line. This time she got right to the point with carefully chosen words and a definite plan to override the irrevocable edict of Haman.

Her emotions seemed to rise as she pleaded with Ahasuerus to overrule Haman's dispatches. "For how can I bear to see the calamity that is coming to my people? Or how can I bear to see the destruction of my kindred?" (8:6). She sounded like a wife who said to her husband, "If you really love me, you will care how I feel and do something about it." He assured her that he did care by reminding her and Mordecai what he had already done. "Behold, I have given Esther the house of Haman, and they have hanged him on the gallows, because he intended to lay hands on the Jews" (8:7).

Esther appealed to the king's favor and the pleasure she brought him. Have you tried that approach with one in authority over you? Have you said to your husband, "Thank you for providing for me and for loving me. I wonder if you could help me with something. I want my time to be free when you are home so that I can enjoy you. Would you help me organize my time?" Are you ready to hear what might displease him and make amends as needed and appropriate for you as a Christian? Husbands, are you ready to help your wife if she has such a request without trying to control her every thought and action?

A New Edict (8:8–14)

Haman was gone, but the edict still remained. The king could not revoke Haman's edict, but he gave Esther permission to write a new irrevocable edict concerning the Jews. Mordecai, wearing the king's signet ring, did not try to invent a new strategy. He used the same resources Haman had (3:12–15). He immediately summoned the scribes to implement Esther's plan. The edict was written to each province in its own script and language in the name of King Ahasuerus and sealed with his signet ring.

No time was wasted. They sent letters by mounted couriers on the king's fastest horses bred from royal studs. The edict was decreed in Susa and every province. It authorized self-defense, annihilation, and plunder of their armed attackers, not aggression toward other people. The Jews were permitted to do the same things to their attackers that Haman's edict had authorized against them on the very day Haman's edict had set for their destruction. Those who would attempt to destroy the Jews would have the same end as Haman. The couriers rode out hurriedly.

Joyful Celebration (8:15–17)

Esther's plan and provision for her people were cause for celebration. Mordecai left the king's presence dressed in royal robes and wearing a great golden crown. Susa rang with shouts of joy. From mourning in sackcloth and ashes, the Jews "had light and gladness and joy and honor" (8:16). "And in every province and in every city, wherever the king's command and his edict reached, there was gladness and joy among the Jews, a feast and a holiday. And many from the peoples of the country declared themselves Jews, for fear of the Jews had fallen on them" (8:17). Possibly some were genuine converts who escaped judgment by uniting with God's people. Can you hear the news spread? "Do not mess with God's people! One of their own, Mordecai, is wielding his power." As in the Exodus and conquest of Canaan,

God gave his people favor with their enemies and filled the surrounding peoples with fear of the Jews.

It is not clear if the Jews were grateful to God or if they were just rejoicing for being saved from destruction. It is proper to celebrate deliverance from danger and harm. However, true celebration recognizes God's grace and power on your behalf, ushering in joyful expressions of gratitude to him.

Truth: The Proper Object of Joyful Gratitude Is God, Not Just His Blessings

What are your thoughts and emotions as you remember God's provision of salvation through Christ's sacrificial death on the cross? How often do you joyfully thank God? Are you filled with gratitude and joy each time you remember Christ's sacrificial death in the Lord's Supper? How do you celebrate God's gift of your salvation? What might you begin to do individually and in your family or circle of friends?

Destruction of the Jews' Enemies (9:1–19)

Imagine the surprise of the Jews' enemies, who expected an easy victory. Instead, they found themselves no match for the Jews, "for the fear of them had fallen on all peoples" (9:2). What produced this fear? The officials, satraps, governors, and royal agents helped the Jews for fear of Mordecai, whose greatness, fame, and increasing power had spread throughout the empire. Behind Mordecai's stature was the God of the Jews, the Holy One of Israel. The Jews in the provinces destroyed their enemies but took no plunder. They were content with defending themselves.

However, the destruction in Susa was incomplete. The Jews killed and destroyed five hundred men and the sons of Haman

(9:12). The king reported to Esther the number of the dead and asked if she had any further request. Esther asked for one more day for the Jews to defend themselves in Susa. Ambitious plotters carrying out the first edict might threaten her and Mordecai. She also asked the king to hang Haman's sons on the gallows. It was common practice to wipe out the family of a conspirator publicly to deter others who might plot against the king and the Jews.[1] Her request explains the different dates for celebrating the Jews' deliverance—the fourteenth of Adar in the villages and the fifteenth of Adar in Susa. At last, the Jews could celebrate with gladness and gifts. The threat of their destruction was over.

Truth: Finishing God's Task for You Inaugurates Peace and Joy

God's people today are faced with the ongoing battle against spiritual forces. These spiritual forces are sin, the worldview that ignores or objects to God, the Devil and his forces, and our own sinful desires. We are not given authority or power to defeat the world or the Devil and his forces, but we can pray to God who alone has power over them and use God's Word as Jesus did when tempted to sin (Matthew 4:1–11). We are commanded to "fight the good fight of the faith" (1 Timothy 6:12) and "be strong in the Lord and in the strength of his might. Put on the whole armor of God, that you may be able to stand against the schemes of the devil" (Ephesians 6:10–11). According to James 4:7, we are not to attack the Devil as though we could defeat him. Instead, we first submit ourselves to God. Then we can resist the devil, and he will flee from us.

---

1. Study note on Esther 9:11–15 in the *ESV® Study Bible* (Wheaton, IL: Crossway, 2008).

While we are to depend on God, victory over specific sin does not mean, "Let go and let God." The New Testament uses words like *strive, fight, make every effort*, and *press on* in exhorting Christians to put off sin and put on Christ's righteousness in daily life. This is the power over sin that Christ has won for his people through his sacrificial death and resurrection. Struggling with sin is a lifelong process because sinful habits do not die easily. Sin has a lingering effect, keeping you in bondage to what you do not destroy. Fighting our flesh can be like pulling out nutgrass in our flowerbeds. The fragile, hair-like roots grow from small round tubers called nutlets. The roots grow deep in the ground and seem to have no end. If you try to pull or dig out the grass, the fragile roots break and you have the grass in your hand, but each nut under the break remains in the ground and forms a new plant. Any effort to thin out the grass results in its multiplication! Likewise, resilient sin crops up after you thought it was gone. Your sin also affects others near you. It is similar to oak wilt in our area. One tree affects those around it because their roots are intertwined.

When God convicts you of a specific sin, confess it—agree with God that it is sin. What sin are you striving to destroy? You cannot win this battle in your own strength. Nevertheless, you must strive, fight, and make every effort in the power of the Holy Spirit to defeat the hold this sin has on your life. Do not be discouraged. Jesus sympathizes with your struggle and intercedes on your behalf in it (Hebrews 4:15; 7:25). Will you press on, asking God each day to help you in this struggle? Remember to thank God for each victory. Trust his promise to forgive that sin and to cleanse you from all unrighteousness (1 John 1:9). The results will be peace with God, yourself, and others, as well as overwhelming gratitude and joy.

New Life for the Jews (9:20–10:3)

Celebration: The Feast of Purim (9:20–32)

As a result of the Jews' salvation and deliverance, they began a new life in Persia. From turmoil and threats, they lived in peace and joy. Esther and Mordecai established the Feast of Purim to remember their deliverance. The celebration would be the same throughout the empire, bringing unity and peace between rural and urban Jewish communities. The name *Purim* is plural for *Pur,* the name of the lot Haman repeatedly cast to determine when to crush and destroy the Jews (3:7). Proverbs 16:33 reminds us again of God's providence: "The lot is cast into the lap, but its every decision is from the LORD." The *ESV Study Bible* says, "The spontaneous celebrations of vv. 16–19 gave way to a properly organized, annual festival."[2]

The Feast of Purim was to be celebrated throughout generations. The Jews accepted their obligations according to what Mordecai had written. The celebration of Purim today is a unified expression of gratitude for the deliverance of the Jews in Persia. The *NIV Archaeology Study Bible* says, "Purim joined the existing five Jewish feasts that had been commanded by Moses in the Torah. Rather than having been prescribed by God's command, this celebration began as a spontaneous response to his covenant faithfulness. Purim is still celebrated today. The entire book of Esther is read in the synagogue on the holiday, during which noisemakers are used. People cheer at the sound of Mordecai's name and boo and hiss at the mention of Haman."[3] The spontaneous joy and gladness expressed

2. Ibid., study note on Esther 9:20–32.
3. Study note on Esther 9:29–32 in the *NIV Archaeological Study Bible* (Grand Rapids: Zondervan, 2005).

by the people became an organized annual tradition in every Jewish community.

What does Purim have to do with God's people, Christians, today? It reminds us that after turmoil, fasting, and lamenting, it is right and imperative to set aside times to remember God's protection and deliverance with joy. It warns us not to omit God from the celebration.

Truth: A Grateful Heart Expresses Thanks to God for His Protection and Deliverance

What spontaneous celebrations of thanksgiving have you experienced personally and in your church? Have you held special services devoted to prayers of praise and thanksgiving? When our church plant welcomed our pastor to our city, we had a "Pie Party" to celebrate God's goodness in providing him and his family to lead us. There was much rejoicing among our group. How might you, your family, and your friends celebrate God's faithfulness to you? How could your church give thanks for God's faithfulness to them? What can you do to be careful to keep God and his deliverance the central reason for celebrating? Our family has a tradition for Easter lunch that began forty years ago. We celebrate Jesus with a cake that looks like a lamb to remind us of the Lamb of God who took away our sin; the empty plate after the cake is eaten reminds us of the tomb that was empty after Jesus' resurrection. What do you do to remember what God has done for you in Christ?

Honor: The Greatness of Mordecai (10:1–3)

The turmoil was over; peace had settled in for Esther, Mordecai, and the Jews. The king imposed taxes reversing the temporary remission that was part of celebrating Esther's crowning (2:18).[4] Again we read about the book of the chronicles of the kings of Media and Persia. He still enjoyed reading about his power and might. However, the full account of the high honor given Mordecai was now complete. He was "second in rank to King Ahasuerus . . . great among the Jews and popular with the multitude of his brothers" (10:3). What made Mordecai so popular? Completely unlike Haman, Mordecai worked for the good of his people. He brought a welcome message of peace.

Truth: God's Measure of Greatness Is Humility

Jesus said that true greatness is in serving, not in being served (Mark 10:44–45). Peter wrote, "Clothe yourselves, all of you, with humility toward one another, for 'God opposes the proud but gives grace to the humble.' Humble yourselves, therefore, under the mighty hand of God so that at the proper time he may exalt you, casting all your anxieties on him, because he cares for you" (1 Peter 5:5b–7).

Esther and Mordecai faced an impossible situation, risking their lives to save their people from destruction. In the end, God exalted them to positions of authority in the kingdom and great service to him and his people.

Esther and Mordecai were ordinary people until God called them to play an integral role in the rescue of his people from destruction. Their daily lives changed dramatically as God began to change the place where they lived, the people in power there, and their own role in Persian life. Entering the contest to be the queen must have seemed strange to a Jewish orphan girl living in exile. Winning the king's favor must have seemed surreal. God

4. Ibid., study note on Esther 10:1.

moves in mysterious ways as he works all things to accomplish his plan and purposes for his people and his glory.

What impossible task are you facing in your personal life, your work, or your family? A broken relationship, a marriage that seems impossible to repair, terminal illness, overwhelming debt, a call to overseas missions, a responsibility in your church? Letting go of everything to place your trust in Jesus Christ? Has God asked you to do something for him, but you cannot even talk to anyone about it? Does God seem to be silent, and yet you see his providence? Perhaps it is for such a time as this that God made you. He will be glorified as you prove the sufficiency of his grace and experience his power that is perfected in your weakness (2 Corinthians 12:9).

He expects you to obey him with humility, drawing from your new life in Christ Jesus. To please God, you will be called upon to die to yourself, depending on his mighty power instead of your own. Dying to self is central to living as a Christian and bearing fruit in Christ's kingdom. That may mean the death of your ambitions, emotions, desires, and plans. It is in dying that you really live. It is in trusting God for the impossible that you really know him, glorify him, and enjoy him. This is the chief end of all those who have been saved by Jesus Christ.

Trusting God may not involve some big task to accomplish. It may be living for his glory in your normal life or in unusual activities and places. He calls his people to live by faith, believing his Word and living in light of it for his honor and glory.

Sharon and David received news that their daughter Kelli had an acute form of cancer. Talk about trusting God was not enough; moment by moment their family was clinging to him. They experienced a new level of joy in the Lord through more than a year of hospitalization, tests, and treatments.

From November 27 to December 9, 2014, Kelli and her family entered a journey that included a new road, a new vocabulary, new surroundings, a new "normal," and a greater empathy for others. December 10, Kelli got the call no one wants to get—the diagnosis was acute myeloid leukemia (AML). Kelli was at the point of death except for the hope of a donor. "Life in the blood" took on a deeper meaning for this family.

In and out of the hospital, she and her family were called to trust God in new ways. Her mother, Sharon, explained that they thought, "When we get past this crisis, things will get better." Instead, they learned that things got different. They experienced how their church works like the body of Christ. They also learned to avoid spending all their time asking questions about percentages, counts, and other technical language whose answers do not have a "God factor."

God's providence has been clear, and his hand has been so far ahead of anywhere they needed to go. When Sharon discovered she was pregnant with Jennifer, Kelli was only six months old. Way back then, God set in motion the provision of a donor for Kelli and a source of comfort for Sharon.

God has been their trip planner, and he had a few surprises along the way. Shortly before the cancer diagnosis, God gave Kelli a new job with a small family-owned business. Her employer paid 100 percent of health insurance for his employees. He told Kelli, "There will always be a job here for you." He is keeping her on the payroll without pay but is paying her insurance premiums.

Jennifer wrote, "I have been meditating on Isaiah 26:3—'You will keep in perfect peace him whose mind is steadfast, because he trusts in you' [1984 NIV]. When my mind is steadfast and I am experiencing God's perfect peace, my mind does not wonder or wander. I am praying we can all continue to be steadfast, focusing on God and his provision without wondering about what's next, if this or that, etc., and without wandering to 'what ifs' or 'maybes'."

One year later, Kelli has completed many tests, chemotherapy, and a successful stem cell transplant with her sister Jennifer the donor. She is grateful to be back at work. While things are generally progressing with Kelli, ongoing appointments at the clinic and with doctors present opportunities for her and her family to rest in the providence and loving care of God. The family has found hope in knowing the last chapter has been written, as Kelli is God's child through faith in his Son, the Lord Jesus Christ.

No one expected what happened March 14, 2016. The leukemia had returned with ferocious intensity. The family received the news that Kelli's time on earth was short. Sharon's remarks about the final days reflect their walk of faith as they waited for God's providential time to call his child home:

"God gave me a sweet gift on the day he took Kelli home. When the medical people put in place the plan of keeping Kelli comfortable with no other medical treatments, I thought Kelli would be gone from here quickly; but that is not what happened. We asked Kelli to wait for her brother, Tim, to get here from Colorado if she could, and she graciously did that. Once he arrived we all told her how much we loved her and gave her permission to quit fighting and go home. She stayed around and her numbers continued to be about the same—several times one of those vital numbers would drop significantly and we would gather around her to love her one more time. Each time she settled and her numbers returned to the same level as before—it seemed she was telling us that she loved having us all close together and she would stay a while longer. I was frustrated that God seemed to be delaying her departure and couldn't understand why he would do that. I now know it was because he had something better planned—something that was way beyond anything I could ever think or imagine to ask him to do.

"Kelli was moved back to her old hospital home—the 8th floor. After she was settled, many of the nurses and her doctor came by to tell her they loved her. Nurse Kelly came in to check on us. As we stood around Kelli's bed, Jenn said, 'Mom, you can get in bed with Kelli now if you want.' This was something I had wanted to do in the ICU, but it had not seemed feasible in that bed. I had often gotten into bed with Kelli in the hospital, and we had watched TV together or did something else together. I climbed in beside Kelli, pulled up the covers, and put my arm around her. Jenn was right beside the bed and Kelli's head was turned so that Jenn could see her face better than I could. Immediately Jenn told me that Kelli's breathing had slowed considerably. Then Kelli took four or five more breaths and left her earthly body—a very peaceful departure.

"My immediate thoughts were that having me beside her was what she had been waiting for. She was right where she began her life—next to me. There we were: the nurse who had lovingly cared for her many times during the past year, her mother who had given her life in the beginning, her sister who had given her life the second time, and God, who had created her, now giving her eternal life!"

Now to him who is able to do far more abundantly than all that we ask or think, according to the power at work within us, to him be glory in the church and in Christ Jesus throughout all generations, forever and ever. Amen. (Ephesians 3:20–21)

"To God be the glory, great things He has done!"[5]

As they thank God for his protection and loving care of their family, he opens their eyes to see other reasons to give thanks. They are resting in his providence, sometimes with tears of both sorrow and joy filling their eyes. They are experiencing their chief end: "Man's chief end is to glorify God and enjoy him forever" (Westminster Shorter Catechism, Answer 1).

The one who offers thanksgiving as his sacrifice glorifies me;
to one who orders his way rightly
I will show the salvation of God!" (Psalm 50:23)

How big is your God? He is with you. He cares. He providentially shows his loving hand to those who look to him for comfort and strength. He will work on your behalf for his glory and the eternal good of others. Living by faith in God will open your eyes to see and embrace his invisible, providential hand at work. You will be filled with gratitude as you prove his faithfulness each day. The fruit of such a life is love, joy, peace, patience, kindness, goodness, faithfulness, gentleness, and self-control (Galatians 5:22–23). To God be the glory for the great things he has done and is doing as he providentially works in and through his people.

5. Fanny Crosby, "To God Be the Glory Great Things He Has Done," 1875.

Poem: "My Life of Faith"

My life of faith is not just "looking back at what was or has
been."
My life of faith is "looking ahead at what is not yet but
will be."
My life of faith is not "knowing all that lies ahead and so
being confident."
My life of faith is "not knowing what lies ahead and yet
being confident of God's presence with me."
My life of faith is not "one mountaintop experience after
another."
My life of faith is "walking through valleys one step at a
time."
My life of faith is not about "having my way."
My life of faith is about "God's having his way with me."
My life of faith is about "enjoying God more than his
blessings."
My life of faith is about "worshiping God for the splendor
of his holiness."
My life of faith is about "glorifying God and enjoying him
forever."

—JANE ROACH, FEBRUARY 7, 1998

Closing Prayer

Lord God, I praise you for your providence and sovereign rule
over your creation. Your wisdom, grace, love, and power open
my eyes to see your hand at work in history, the present world
conditions, and my own life. Give me grace to live by faith in

your presence with me and in your providential outworking of your plan in my life. Increase my desire for you and your Word. Help me to be faithful to continue the habit of daily Bible study that I may know you better, love you more deeply, and serve you with unwavering commitment. Let me celebrate with joy the deliverance from sin that is mine in Christ Jesus, your Son and my Lord. For your honor and glory. Amen.

Joyful Worship

These days should be remembered . . . (Esther 9:28)

Oh come, let us worship and bow down; let us kneel before the LORD, our Maker! (Psalm 95:6)

Text

Esther 1–10

Truths

God's chief end is to display his glory. "Man's chief end is to glorify God and enjoy him forever" (Westminster Shorter Catechism, Answer 1).

Hymn: "God Moves in a Mysterious Way"

God moves in a mysterious way
His wonders to perform;
He plants his footsteps in the sea,
And rides upon the storm.

Deep in unfathomable mines
Of never-failing skill
He treasures up his bright designs,
And works his sovereign will.

Ye fearful saints, fresh courage take;
The clouds ye so much dread
Are big with mercy, and shall break
In blessings on your head.

Judge not the Lord by feeble sense,
But trust him for his grace;
Behind a frowning providence
He hides a smiling face.

His purposes will ripen fast,
Unfolding ev'ry hour;
The bud may have a bitter taste,
But sweet will be the flow'r.

Blind unbelief is sure to err,
And scan his work in vain;
God is his own interpreter,
And he will make it plain.

—WILLIAM COWPER, 1774

After completing a Bible study, it behooves us to stop and worship God for the truth he has revealed to us, especially about himself. Throughout the book of Esther, we have seen the invisible hand of God's providence that will not allow the

240

covenant people to be utterly destroyed or God's eternal plan to be thwarted. Let us take time to record what we have learned and worship God for his truth and its action in our lives. *The New Matthew Henry Commentary* points out,

> God does not deal with us according to our foolishness and weakness. Those Jews who were scattered in the provinces of the nations were taken care of, just as those who gathered in the land of Judea were. They were wonderfully preserved when doomed to destruction and appointed as sheep to be slaughtered (Ps 44:22). It is the record of a plot against the Jews to destroy them all. The name of God is not found in this book . . . but the finger of God is, directing many minute events to bring about the rescue of his people.[1]

For each of the upcoming reviews, follow these instructions:

- List the ways in Esther you see God working behind the scenes in specific details to remain faithful to his people and to rescue them from destruction.
- Write an example of how God has worked similarly in your life.
- Select a word or phrase from "God Moves in a Mysterious Way" that illustrates this example from your life.
- Write a brief prayer of thanksgiving for God's providence in history and your life.
- If you are part of a group study, bring your responses to the final class to contribute to the corporate worship of God.

1. Martin H. Manser, ed., *The New Matthew Henry Commentary* (Grand Rapids: Zondervan, 2010), 588.

A New Queen for Persia

▶ REVIEW ESTHER 1–2

God makes a way for Esther to become queen. Mordecai's good service for the king in discovering a plot against his life is recorded but goes unnoticed by the king.

- God's providence in Esther

- God's providence in my life in a similar way

- A word or phrase from "God Moves in a Mysterious Way" that relates to this expression of God's providence in my life

- Prayer of thanksgiving

A Frightening New Edict

▶ REVIEW ESTHER 3

Enraged by Mordecai's refusal to give him honor, Haman deceitfully gains an order for the destruction of all the Jews in Persia.

- God's providence in Esther

- God's providence in my life

- A word or phrase from "God Moves in a Mysterious Way" that relates to this expression of God's providence in my life

- Prayer of thanksgiving

A Plan to Stop the Genocide

▶ REVIEW ESTHER 4

Mordecai, Esther, and the Jews unite in a plan to stop the genocide of the Jews.

• God's providence in Esther

• God's providence in my life

- A word or phrase from "God Moves in a Mysterious Way" that relates to this expression of God's providence in my life

- Prayer of thanksgiving

A Wise, Bold Queen Esther

▶ REVIEW ESTHER 5

Esther boldly and courageously approaches the king with patience and humility while arrogant Haman plots to hang Mordecai.

- God's providence in Esther

- God's providence in my life

- A word or phrase from "God Moves in a Mysterious Way" that relates to this expression of God's providence in my life

- Prayer of thanksgiving

Honoring the One He Wants to Kill

▶ REVIEW ESTHER 6

The king's insomnia and the record of Mordecai's service turn the tables for humiliated Haman, who gives humble Mordecai the honor arrogant Haman desired for himself.

• God's providence in Esther

• God's providence in my life

- A word or phrase from "God Moves in a Mysterious Way" that relates to this expression of God's providence in my life

- Prayer of thanksgiving

The Murderous Plot Revealed

▶ REVIEW ESTHER 7

Esther pleads with the king to save her people and reveals Haman as the villain who seals his doom by his own folly.

- God's providence in Esther

- God's providence in my life

- A word or phrase from "God Moves in a Mysterious Way" that relates to this expression of God's providence in my life

- Prayer of thanksgiving

A New Beginning

▶ REVIEW ESTHER 8–10

Esther is honored, Haman is hanged, and Mordecai is promoted. The general plot against the Jews is defeated and remembered forever in the Feast of Purim.

• God's providence in Esther

• God's providence in my life

- A word or phrase from "God Moves in a Mysterious Way" that relates to this expression of God's providence in my life

- Prayer of thanksgiving

For Such a Time as This

1. Why does God involve his people rather than just acting by himself?

2. Where is God giving you an opportunity to be involved in spreading truth about him and the Lord Jesus Christ? How will you respond?

Closing Prayer

Sovereign, almighty, providential God, to glorify you is to enjoy you. You have graciously revealed your glory through the book of Esther. You have opened my mind to know more of your providence. You have moved the knowledge from my head to my heart, causing me to appreciate your sovereign control of all of life. But you have done far more than that. You have given me love that I did not have before, so that I now embrace your sovereignty and providence in all of life and in the minute details of my own life. I recognize your mysterious ways that were previously hidden. I delight in seeing how you have previously been where I now am, preparing the way for me in relationships, ministry, and joyful worship. May you find joy in giving me courage, peace, wisdom, and faith. To you alone belongs the glory. Amen.

Recommended Reading

Duguid, Iain M. *Esther & Ruth*. Reformed Expository Commentary. Phillipsburg, NJ: P&R Publishing, 2005.

Gaebelein, Frank E., ed. *1 & 2 Kings, 1 & 2 Chronicles, Ezra, Nehemiah, Esther, Job*. The Expositor's Bible Commentary, vol. 4. Grand Rapids: Zondervan, 1988.

Hannah, John D. *To God Be the Glory*. Today's Issues. Wheaton, IL: Crossway Books, 2000.

Henry, Matthew. *The New Matthew Henry Commentary*. Edited by Martin H. Manser. Grand Rapids: Zondervan, 2010.

Kaiser, Walter C., Jr., and Duane Garret, eds. *NIV Archaeological Study Bible: An Illustrated Walk Through Biblical History and Culture*. Grand Rapids: Zondervan, 2005.

Keller, Timothy. "Esther and the Hiddenness of God." Sermons delivered from April 15, 2007 to May 6, 2007. www.gospelinlife.com /esther-and-the-hiddenness-of-god.

Orr, James, ed. *The International Standard Bible Encyclopedia*. Chicago: The Howard-Severance Company, 1915. (This public domain resource can be found at www.biblestudytools.com.)

Tenney, Merrill C., ed. *The Zondervan Pictorial Encyclopedia of the Bible*, vol. 5. Grand Rapids: Zondervan, 1976.

Thomas, Derek W. H. *What Is Providence?* Basics of the Faith. Phillipsburg, NJ: P&R Publishing, 2008.

Tozer, A. W. *The Pursuit of God*. Camp Hill, PA: Christian Publications, 1982.

Walvoord, John F., and Roy B. Zuck, eds. *The Bible Knowledge Commentary: Old Testament*. Wheaton, IL: Victor Books, 1985.